SUPER
VILLAINS

•W.H.JOHNSON•

COUNTRYSIDE BOOKS
NEWBURY, BERKSHIRE

First published 2004
© W. H. Johnson 2004

COUNTRYSIDE BOOKS
3 Catherine Road
Newbury, Berkshire

To view our complete range of books,
please visit us at
www.countrysidebooks.co.uk

ISBN 1 85306 852 7

Designed by Peter Davies, Nautilus Design
Produced through MRM Associates Ltd., Reading
Typeset by Mac Style Ltd, Scarborough, N. Yorkshire
Printed by J.W. Arrowsmith Ltd., Bristol

Contents

ACKNOWLEDGEMENTS

———— ✿ ————

I am grateful to the following people who have been extremely helpful to me while I have been writing this book.

Several former senior police officers have given advice. As on a previous occasion Bob Bartlett has made a number of excellent suggestions and John Lister was of significant assistance when I came to write the chapter about the Cracknell kidnap. Tony Forward's help was also welcome. And Alan Skinner, formerly a member of the Sussex force, was able to find information for me that might otherwise have proved difficult.

I am indebted to the Press Office of the Surrey Police for pictures of the Motocross gang and to Sandra Leeming of Fulcrum TV for the transcript of their programme on the Cutt Mill murder. My thanks go to Liza Kearney of Woking Online for tracing Nicholas Hilliard whose relative was at the centre of the Lower Knaphill affair. I am grateful to Nicholas for his help in checking the draft chapter. Iain Wakeford of Woking kindly allowed me to use his photograph of Nuthurst where the events in this case unfolded.

I thank my old friend David Riddick, the Garrick of Worth, for his assistance and particularly for his navigational skills in tracking down two of the more elusive sites. And similar sincere thanks go to my wife Anne for her patience and for the critical eye she has brought to this book, to my other books and in fact to most of my activities.

AREA MAP OF SURREY

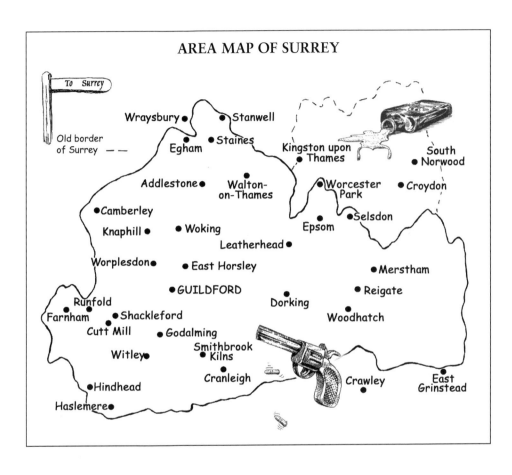

INTRODUCTION

———— ✿ ————

Surrey can congratulate itself on its great good fortune in having – or at least appearing to have – less criminal activity than any other English county. Nevertheless, I have collected here a gallery of villains to match any in the land. I have tried to vary their activities so that among them there are stick-up men and racecourse razor gangs, a white collar fraudster and a poisoner. As a matter of fact I'm pretty sure that there are a couple of other poisoners in here though you'll have to make up your own mind on that. And there is a mercifully unsuccessful hitman side by side with the first of the supergrasses.

Of course, not all of the villains in this book lived in Surrey. Several, such as Richard Brinkley and the racecourse gangs, simply came visiting, did their dirty work and left. Others, like the Lerwills, resided in the county for only a short time. Bertie Smalls was living in Selsdon at the time of his arrest though there is no evidence of his having committed any offences in the county.

And the purists may quibble about the boundaries of my Surrey. What have Croydon and Kingston to do with Surrey, they may ask. Well, yes, there have been numerous boundary changes over the years but I know that many in the Outer London boroughs still believe themselves to be in the county. And so I have taken some licence in the matter. I hope that readers will excuse this.

Above all, I hope that readers will find these accounts of Surrey villains entertaining and interesting. I think it safe to say that in the majority of cases they have not previously appeared in book form. I think they merit a close look.

W.H. Johnson

THE KIDNAPPING OF VICTOR CRACKNELL

———————— ✿ ————————

Where was he? Would he ever get away from here, wherever it was? How could he, trussed up in a tightly zipped sleeping bag like this? On the first night torrential rain had soaked the bag and ever since, Victor had lain in the damp, the raw cold edging into his bones. No good struggling. He had been warned of what might happen if he did. He would strangle himself for there was a thick wire around his neck and this extended to a tree to which it was secured by small bolts. If he struggled the noose would pull tighter until it throttled him. From time to time the man visited him, gave him scraps of food and cold drinks, made threats.

Yesterday – or was it the day before? – Victor had struggled and had managed to remove his blindfold but he could not escape from the sleeping bag. When the man came back and saw that he had been trying to release himself he had produced an electric cattle prod and had touched him with it several times. If he tried to escape again, his captor told him, he would be electrocuted.

So the 32 year old prisoner lay there, out in the open, hour after hour, day after day, absolutely helpless, gagged, his ears plugged with plasticine, his eyes taped, hooded, and handcuffed. And wondered about home. Wondered about Deborah and the boys. Wondered if the police were involved yet. Wondered whether they would ever find him. Wondered if he really was to be killed.

Over and over Victor played the journey through his head, the car ride after he had been taken from home, during the night, following an ever so normal August Sunday. He'd been bundled into his own car and after only half a mile or so had been transferred to another vehicle. Then for several hours he had been forced to lie on the floor of the car with his hands cuffed behind him, as his kidnapper drove him, blind and mute, he knew not where.

When they finally came to a halt, he was taken out of the car in this isolated place with its wind and rain and silence and marched here, where he was made to get into the sleeping bag, which was then tightly zipped. He was warned that he would die, would strangle to death, if he tried to escape. But how could he get away, tethered as he was?

He knew what it was all about – he was a kidnap victim. It was an attempt to extort money from his father, Desmond Cracknell, the multi-millionaire businessman, chairman of the family company, Food Brokers Ltd, one of Britain's biggest privately owned firms and now, in 1989, Europe's largest food-brokerage firm.

Victor had been told about the ransom demands. And told too what would happen to him if the money was not forthcoming. He would be killed. It was so absurd, the stuff of movies, the kind of thing that didn't happen in real life. Not to people in Surrey. Not in East Horsley. You got break-ins there from time to time as you did in all wealthy stockbroker-belt locations but not kidnappings, not death threats. And yet here he was in this remote spot. Only hours earlier they'd been in bed and had been awakened when the light went on suddenly. They couldn't believe it, he and Deborah. There was a man standing there in the bedroom wearing a black balaclava, dark sunglasses and army fatigues and carrying a sawn-off shotgun. A burglar? So it seemed at first. He was after money he told them. They had no need to be afraid, he said, he wouldn't hurt them if they did as they were told.

How could they resist an armed man? There were the four boys in the house, the eldest only six years old, the youngest a baby. They just had to do as they were told. Victor was ordered to dress himself and then Deborah was instructed to handcuff him and blindfold him with sticking plaster. Then, with the gun pressed to her face, she was handcuffed to the dressing table.

The man helped himself to money and credit cards and then made it obvious that Victor was being kidnapped as he was led out of the house at gunpoint. 'If you want to see your husband alive again,' he told Deborah, 'pay the ransom.'

Before leaving he took a sheet of paper, a ransom note, out of his pocket and placed it on the dressing table.

And only minutes later Deborah heard the car, Victor's BMW 320i, drive away.

It was seven hours before Deborah managed to release herself. The children were in the house but rather than waken them and frighten them with her calls she struggled to free herself, alone with her anxiety. At last she was able to telephone her father-in-law to whom the note was obviously directed.

The ransom note made it clear that should any attempt be made to contact the police or the media Victor's life would be in danger. 'If you want your son free without harm you pay one million fine in 10 pounds, 20 pounds, 50 pounds notes in 3 days your son perhaps lose finger as example for you maybe he lose ear or nose as well if we do think you cheat if instructions not followed ...'

Broken English perhaps but explicit enough.

And there was no time to waste, that was clear. Payment was to be made by one o'clock on Thursday morning. In less than 76 hours. And if it was not forthcoming, mutilation. And death. And the police were not to be informed.

But despite his daughter-in-law's misgivings, Desmond Cracknell had no hesitation in contacting the police. Within an hour the house was under surveillance and the telephones tapped.

Kidnapping is a rare crime in Britain and it was Surrey police force's first case of this kind. At once the Chief Constable, Brian Hayes, sought help from the Metropolitan Police, several of whose officers had received training with the FBI in how to deal with kidnapping, blackmail and extortion.

The Yard's advice to the Surrey officers, led by Detective Superintendent John Milner, was to stay calm and try to play for time. It was unlikely, they said, that the kidnapper would kill his victim as long as he thought that he had a chance of getting the ransom money. The moment when he went to collect the money would be the kidnapper's most vulnerable time. This would offer a chance to the police to follow the culprit in the hope that he would lead them to Victor.

Milner's team wondered about the authenticity of the roughly typed ransom note. On the face of it they were dealing with some kind of international terrorist group, identifying themselves on the note as The People's Revolutionary Group Active Service Unit and accusing Desmond Cracknell of being 'an enemy of the people'. The threats to kill or mutilate Victor unless the £1m ransom was paid by Thursday at one o'clock in the morning were couched in halting English. There certainly were ruthless organisations capable of such brutal responses if they were thwarted. If Victor Cracknell had fallen into the clutches of such a group who could foretell what might happen to him? Were they foreigners? Or perhaps the IRA? However, right from the beginning Detective Superintendent Milner doubted that political terrorists were involved and a crime profiler who inspected the note was of the same opinion. But was this a lone kidnapper or was he a member of a gang?

With time pressing, the police had no idea who had taken Victor Cracknell nor where he might be by now. The BMW that had been driven off from the Cracknells' East Horsley home had been found at the local station. Obviously the kidnapper had had another getaway car waiting there, but this was not significantly helpful to the police. At this early stage they knew so little. It was a matter of waiting for the kidnapper to make contact.

Fearing that publicity about the case might endanger Victor's safety, crime reporters from Fleet Street and national TV were summoned by the Chief Constable to Surrey police headquarters at Guildford. They agreed to a news blackout and in consequence no references to the kidnapping were made in any of the media.

No one was told of the kidnap save a few senior executives in the business. And the family was encouraged to behave as normally as possible during this difficult period. The three older children, Peter, Richard and Simon, unaware of what had happened to their father, continued to play their summer holiday games with other children near their home. One neighbour said later: 'The boys were out each day and if they knew anything was wrong, they did not say anything or give any hint of it.'

Although there were police officers in the house to guide him through any negotiations, it was always Desmond who answered the telephone calls. He was the man the kidnapper expected to deal with. Unsurprisingly, there were phone taps on all incoming calls to the Cracknell household.

The first phone call, which lasted no more than 15 seconds, came on Tuesday afternoon. A man introduced himself to Desmond as Mr Murphy. He confirmed that the money was to be made ready in used notes in £10, £20 and £50 denominations. Desmond was given a contact number, with an agreed code word, to use in telephone kiosks at motorway service stations throughout the South and Midlands. It seemed that it was going to be one of those run-around affairs, designed to prevent the possibility of the police intervening, the man with the money being directed to various locations before he handed over the ransom.

Murphy rang again later in the day. Desmond told him that before he negotiated further he had to be reassured that his son was still alive. He asked for answers to two questions to which Victor would know the answer. Murphy rang again later in the day with the correct responses. At this point Desmond, acting on police advice, offered £130,000 for his son's safe release. Murphy, clearly furious at such a pittance, rang off.

On the following day, Murphy telephoned several times, on each occasion becoming more and more impatient and angry at Desmond's insistence that he could not find the money that had been demanded at such short notice. He could only manage £130,000, he told the kidnapper. Desmond was to say later, 'It was a battle of wills. I think in the end we managed to get on top.' Nevertheless he had feared he might never see Victor alive again.

At the same time as these calls were being made, police were tracing them to pay telephones in or west of Bristol.

It was during this time that Desmond received a tape recording of his son's voice. At least it proved that he was still alive but it was also evident that Victor was very frightened by his ordeal.

But the one o'clock deadline passed on the Thursday morning. There was no call from Murphy. Not until afternoon did he make his final telephone call. He would accept a lower sum, he said: £400,000, paid in instalments, was what he now demanded. A first cash-drop of £142,000 was to be left in a clearing in a small wood near a lay-by on the Hog's Back on the A31. And Desmond was to deliver it in person, he was told. Let him remember, any attempt to intercept the courier and Victor would be executed.

Late on the afternoon of Thursday, 16 August, Desmond took the money, packed in a briefcase, to the pick-up point. He was later to admit that this was the most frightening moment of all. What if he were murdered, the money stolen, and then his son done away with? It was, he thought, a possibility.

When Desmond returned home there was another call from Murphy. Where was the money, he asked. Why had it not been delivered? Did Desmond realise the danger he was putting his son in? The matter was quickly cleared up. Desmond explained where he had placed the ransom money. It was not where the kidnapper had expected it to be.

Some time later an Audi drew up in the lay-by and the driver went to the woodland pick-up point. He returned with the briefcase, which he placed in the car-boot and drove off. He was unaware that undercover police from the Surrey force had him under surveillance. For the next three hours the Audi was followed until it arrived at a house in Exeter.

But where was Victor? His father had been told to expect to hear from his son by two o'clock in the morning. But there was nothing. Had the kidnapper reneged on the agreement? Had he settled for £142,000 and done away with his bargaining counter? Throughout the long morning hours the family waited to hear that Victor had been released but there was nothing.

In the meantime, the Surrey policemen, with their colleagues from Devon and Cornwall in support, hesitated to pick up their suspect in case it would jeopardise the kidnapped man's safety.

And then at about lunchtime there was a phone call from Devon. Victor was free. He had, unaware of the negotiations, made his escape from a gully in an obscure moorland spot and was now calling from a farm at Higher Ashton on the edge of Dartmoor. He had concluded that his abductor had abandoned him for there had been no visits for more than a day and he had not eaten for at least 28 hours. Despite the warning that he would strangle himself if he attempted to escape, he felt he had no alternative but to take the risk and he managed, though still handcuffed, to free himself from the sleeping bag and avoid the noose. Now at Lakenheath Farm, distressed and suffering from hypothermia after 96 hours exposure, he was awaiting the arrival of the fire brigade to cut off his handcuffs. It did not matter that his wrists were chafed bright red by the cuffs nor that his face and neck bore red weals from the noose. He was safe. And relieved to be alive. At the outset he had been told that if the ransom money was not forthcoming he would be killed. Small wonder that during all those days of his imprisonment he had been desperately afraid. 'It was', Victor later said, 'thoughts of my family, prayers and a love of life that got me through the ordeal.'

And now, in a joint operation involving armed officers from the Surrey and the Devon and Cornwall forces and two Regional Crime Squads, 40 year old Keith Rose was arrested at a house in Prospect Park in Exeter. Here they found a shotgun and £111,000 in a wardrobe. They quickly established that Rose had had debts of £35,000 and an overdraft of £4,500. And that he was both vicious and fascinating.

Rose had no criminal record and had no intention of becoming a career criminal. He was after one big pay-day. And Desmond Cracknell, he thought, could provide him with this. For he knew well enough about Desmond and his highly successful firm, Food Brokers, who had made household names of products such as Babycham, Jolly Green Giant, Tic Tac Mints and Uncle Ben's Rice. There was money there, enough for the ambitious Keith Rose. At one time, the former public schoolboy had worked for Food Brokers with a responsibility for fruit and vegetables. And they had even given him a poor reference. How dare they? They were the ones who would pay. And then he would succeed, he told himself. He had had bad luck in recent years when he had set up his own businesses, first dealing in detergents wholesale and then computers. At first things had gone well – there'd been the Porsche and the luxury hotels, the flying lessons, the long lunches and the late, late dinners. But then in 1988 things had really gone downhill. The current business collapsed and the days of wine and roses were over. Then his wife left him. And now he found himself living on Social Security and with a second wife. It seemed unfair.

Well, the Cracknells would pay. Because he really wanted a Maserati; he wanted a deer park and a couple of farms and he wanted to buy his new wife a decent diamond ring, something worth in the region of £10,000.

At the Old Bailey in September 1990 Keith Rose faced charges of burglary, the theft of £25, the illegal possession of a shotgun and two sets of handcuffs, assault on Mrs Cracknell and imprisoning her against her will. He was also charged with carrying away Mr Cracknell against his will and assaulting him. After he was found guilty, Mr Justice Pownall described Rose as 'not only vicious, violent and dangerous, but evil, callous and warped'.

'Your offence is aggravated', the judge continued, 'because you planned it over a period and you prepared quite deliberately the deprivation of the dignity of another human being. Blackmail, too, is one of the ugliest crimes in the criminal calendar because it is nothing more or less than attempted murder of the soul ...'

And for that murder of the soul Keith Rose was sentenced to 15 years' imprisonment.

Certainly Rose made his victim suffer extremes of physical and mental anguish. One might reasonably wonder if Victor would ever have been freed had he not got away himself. Was it Rose's intention to leave him in that remote gully in Devon until he starved to death? Was he callous enough to do that? Of course he was. For as a consequence of the Cracknell kidnapping another crime was resolved. Keith Rose turned out to be a murderer quite without conscience.

In September 1981 a 42 year old mother of two, Juliet Rowe, whose husband Gerald had built up a chain of eighteen supermarkets and two bakery shops, had been found in her home at Budleigh Salterton, shot at point blank range. There were four bullets in her back, one in her head and another in her heart. The murder had never been solved. There was no substantial forensic evidence to point to the killer's identity and no apparent motive for the killing. Many wondered if her husband was responsible. He had always claimed that he had been lured to an appointment with a salesman who never arrived and whom police never traced. But the case lay unresolved until the Cracknell kidnapping.

Keith Rose.

Devon and Cornwall Police had conducted extensive interviews in the West Country and had taken 150 pistols to be test-fired. But there was no result. Rose had been lucky. When the police had looked at his .22 pistol, they had given it back to him without test-firing it. But now when Rose was charged with kidnapping his fingerprints were sent by Surrey Police as a matter of routine to the Devon and Cornwall force. And these matched prints taken in the Rowe house after the murder. The investigation into the murder of Juliet Rowe was immediately reopened. A pistol found in Rose's house was inspected (again) and this time identified as the weapon used in the murder.

At about the same time, Gerald Rowe saw an item on the television news and heard a reference to Food Brokers. He recalled being approached in a Devon public house, a month or so before the kidnapping, by a man who asked if he recognised him as a former representative of Food Brokers. When he was responsible for fruit and vegetables? Did he remember him? When he called on him when he was working for the firm? And then came the most astonishing question: 'Did you know I was pulled on your wife's murder because I belonged to a gun club?'

Rowe had dismissed the matter at the time, not remembering having dealt with the man and simply thinking him odd, but now hearing the reference on the news to the kidnapping and Food Brokers he contacted the police. There might be some link, he thought, between the two cases. Perhaps this was not significant in resolving the murder inquiry but it does indicate something of the kind of man the police had in custody.

It was after the murder trial at Exeter that Mr Justice Connell told Rose that he regarded him as 'an evil and exceptionally dangerous man'. The judge went on, 'This is as grave a case of murder as I have ever encountered. You were a lucky man in 1981. It is unfortunate it took far too many years, but your luck has finally run out.' And so it had. He was sentenced to life and is unlikely ever to be released.

There is no doubt that the murder of Juliet Rowe was an attempted kidnap. Rose knew that his victim was married to a wealthy man with whom he had had dealings. He had ensured that Gerald Rowe was away from home and had then gone to the house claiming to be a telephone engineer. Suspicious about her visitor Mrs Rowe had pressed the automatic alarm but by the time the police arrived she lay dead in the hall. In a struggle Rose had shot her, first disabling her. He had then callously, like an executioner, dispatched her with shots to the head and heart.

And it was this man, Keith Rose, who eight years later kidnapped Victor Cracknell. Had it not been for expert work by the police – the superb cooperation that Surrey Constabulary received from the Metropolitan Police, from two Regional Crime Squads and the Devon and Cornwall force was a vital factor in the success of the investigation – and of course his father's cool head, Victor Cracknell might never have returned to his wife and family.

A Day at the Races

———————— ❀ ————————

'Here they come, boys,' says the feller with the binoculars. He's looking up the Epsom road and he spots the Crossley truck on its way up the hill towards them. Only a dozen or so inside, he reckons. All the better. A quiet spot, real country with fields and hedges. Peaceful, you might say. But they'll pay them out this time. Serve them right. Hadn't the Sabinis carved up one of their lads last night at Covent Garden? Hadn't he needed 70 stitches in his legs? And hadn't he suffered other injuries? Just wait.

'Ready, lads?' someone shouts and the car backs out of the side lane and into the road. The Crossley puts the brakes on, slows down, stops.

'What's going on here?' the men in the Crossley ask each other. They've had such a good Derby Day. Not that bookies often have bad Derby Days. And today, Derby Day 1921, even with Steve Donoghue up on Humorist, they've done very well. So what's the hold-up now? They want to get on, back home to Leeds. And some of them clamber out to see what's going on. Bloomin' car just come out the lane, just like that. Stuck right in front of them. But now they see these other fellers, thirty, nearly forty of them, and they're coming at them, coming at the Crossley from the lane. Must have been hiding there, waiting for them. And they hear the shouts, 'Kill the Italians.' And they look as if they are ready to kill somebody because they're all armed to the teeth, carrying hammers, razors, coshes, half bricks, clubs. There's even two or three with guns. And the men in the Crossley don't have a chance. Not against so many of them. So they fight back as best they can but they also try to get away. One of them loses three fingers when a meat cleaver smashes down on his hand. Charlie Swartz is lucky.

Somebody has a swipe at him with a chopper but though he takes a bit of a knock he manages to escape to the lavatory of the nearby Brick Kiln pub. But others are less fortunate and they are carved up with razors, beaten with iron bars, punched with knuckledusters and kicked with heavy duty boots. And at some point the beatings end. The attackers call a halt. Either because they have dished out well-merited punishment or because some slow-dawning truth descends upon them. Perhaps it is when Lazarus Green, running for his life, calls out in desperation, 'What are you doing? We are from Leeds.' And his pursuer halts and reflects on the words he has just heard. From Leeds? 'Blimey!' he says. 'I hope we've not made a mistake. Get into that field and lie down or you'll be killed.'

And they had made a mistake. The Brummagem boys had handed out a merciless beating not to Darby Sabini's mob from Clerkenwell but to the Leeds men, their allies. Something had gone wrong. Somebody had made a mistake. It oughtn't to be the

Italian gangsters from Clerkenwell in 1920. Darby Sabini, with cap and muffler, is immediately behind the seated man.

Leeds boys lying there, with their cheeks slashed, their ears hanging off, their arms broken, their ribs cracked. That wasn't the plan. That wasn't what they intended when they set up the ambush at Ewell.

And now the police were on their way. That much was certain. You could hear their cars clanging their alarms as they raced down from the course. No point in hanging around. No time for apologies. Off they went, the Brummagem boys, in their charabanc. Earlier in the day they had ordered food at the George and Dragon on Kingston Hill. Best be off there. Leaving the Leeds men sprawled by the side of the road, nursing their injuries. Perhaps they were all grateful that no one had been killed.

The Flying Squad were on the scene shortly after the departure of the Brummagem boys. Then the news came that the charabanc had pulled up at the George and Dragon and that the men were in the garden. Very soon 50 police officers surrounded the pub, and Sergeant Merrett ensured that the charabanc would go no further by taking out the sparking plugs. His colleague, Sergeant Dawson, who was armed with a revolver, went into the garden alone, calling out that the men should consider themselves in custody. When some of them stood up and threatened him, the sergeant pulled out the gun. 'I will shoot the first man who moves,' he told them. The suspects caved in and remained where they were until other officers arrived.

Rounding up the gang, the police found Thomas Eivers carrying a fish basket containing two hammers and a loaded Mauser pistol. Other weapons were discovered under seats. Thomas Tuckey was caught trying to hide a loaded Webley revolver. Eventually 28 of about 40 men were under arrest and taken to Kingston police station. However, several of the ringleaders had already escaped.

At Epsom Hospital all of the Leeds men who had been so savagely assaulted were patched up although five of them were detained with severe injuries.

So what was it all about? What was the mistake? Why were the Leeds men, most of them Jewish, mistaken for the Italian mob? Why had they received such a hiding from a gang they had thought were their allies in the murky, brutal world of racetrack politics?

Of course it was all part of the struggle of rival gangsters to control the bookies' pitches. It was about a protection racket and who should run it. It was about Billy Kimber's control of pitches on courses throughout the country and the attempts of the upstart Darby Sabini to wrest it from him. And Billy Kimber, a major underworld figure, an immaculate, charming man when not 'on business', had controlled most of the racecourses, north and south, since 1910. It was his heavies, the Brummagem boys, who stood by the bookmakers' pitches with the hammers in their jacket pockets, visible reminders of their savage reputation – just to let anyone who fancied his chances know that he ran an almighty risk if he trifled with the bookies in Billy Kimber's pocket. It was a ferocious rule and woe betide anyone who dared threaten the Kimber empire.

And what about the law? What about the police and the courts? But significant numbers of racecourse police were in the pay of the rival barons and they turned a blind eye to many an 'indiscretion'. And when they went to court on charges of assault, grievous bodily harm, riot, these gangsters, these ill-educated thugs, many of them unemployed, others painters and labourers, porters and platelayers, were represented in court by the most eminent men in their field. Shootings, stabbings, bookmakers razor-slashed or even thrown into their office fires, jockeys with the wrong result beaten, punters thrown off trains: not all such cases came before the courts but when they did the best legal brains argued their clients' innocence cogently, mildly, with urbane wit and charm.

Not that all of Kimber's followers were from Birmingham. In fact most were Londoners as was Kimber himself and in particular they came from the Elephant and Castle. His gang were perhaps not especially politically inclined although many of them were strongly anti-Semitic, anti-foreigner, and in particular they hated and resented the growing power of the Sabini mob from Little Italy (Clerkenwell and Soho) and their Jewish allies led by Alfie Solomon.

The rise of the Italians – though let it be said that few of them had more than a handful of Italian words handed down from their parents and grandparents – had been sudden and due principally to the cunning and the violent power of Darby Sabini, on whom

Graham Greene would later model the gangster Colleoni in *Brighton Rock*. He was in stark contrast to Billy Kimber. He was no dandy: he was recognised throughout his life by his cloth cap, his modest suit and his white muffler. He was like many another working-class labourer of his time, save of course that he did not labour. Leading his mob was a full-time occupation. Fighting his way against prospective opposition was a way of life. And Sabini imposing his power on the southern racecourses was what so irked Billy Kimber. And it seemed that increasingly the police, including senior members of the Flying Squad, deferred to Sabini rather than Kimber on the courses. In 1920 the Racecourse Bookmakers and Backers Protection Association, which gave formal and quasi-legal protection to bookmakers, was formed. Its stewards, paid £6 a week, were members of the Sabini gang. Such presumption could not be allowed. It was only a matter of time before the two parties clashed seriously. There had of course been fights over the years but now matters were coming to a head. There had been stabbings, shootings, razor-slashings on racecourses and on railway stations, in streets and pubs whenever members of the two gangs met.

In 1921 there were several run-ins. A Birmingham gangster was razor-slashed at London Bridge station. Darby Sabini was attacked by a mob at Greenford. One of his men threw him a gun, which he fired into the ground. In the melée he managed to escape. At Alexandra Park bookies were felled with bottles. Taxi drivers who had driven the Sabinis to the racecourse were attacked and shot. The police at Birmingham were told that there was a plan to bomb a Sabini haunt in London. It was all boiling up ready for Derby Day. And the flames were stoked by Reuben Bigland, the Birmingham tycoon and fraudster, following a complaint by the outrageous Horatio Bottomley, another tricky customer. Bottomley, the owner of *John Bull* magazine, continuing his phoney act as the 'Soldiers' Friend' and the great patriot, had observed to Bigland that it was wrong that Italians like the Sabinis should be depriving 'Our Boys' of a living, particularly after their gallant fight in World War One. He comfortably forgot that most of those he described as Italians had never lived in Italy and that many had served in the British forces.

But Bigland and Bottomley were agreed: what was needed was a punitive expedition. Somehow it looks as if Billy Kimber had official blessing for such an expedition.

And so on the Epsom racecourse on Derby Day, Thursday, 2 June 1921, Billy Kimber watched his enemies as they watched him. And with his principal lieutenants, George Sage and Mad Harry Brown, he planned to ambush the Sabinis on their way home from the course. Everything was quiet during the meeting despite the presence of other mobs from Leeds, Sheffield, Uttoxeter and Hoxton. Nothing happened till the Leeds men were on their way home, motoring along the Epsom road. Then all hell broke out. And their allies, Billy Kimber's men, all but murdered them. By mistake. How had it happened that way? How was it that not long afterwards 28 of them faced charges at Surrey Assizes at Guildford charged with conspiring to commit and committing grievous bodily harm to a group of men from Leeds – Charles Swartz, Lazarus Green, Joseph Cohen, David Robinson, Solomon Levison, Michael Lewis, Isaac Lewis, Herbert Whiteley, Sam Barnett and Jack Morris? Ironic that. The majority of these were Jewish. The Brummagem boys were normally dead set against Jews but at that time both parties were in alliance against the Sabini mob. But Darby Sabini had made his plans too.

At the end of the race meeting the Leeds men had gone to the coach park and found that their bus would not start. They were unaware that one of the Sabinis had removed the rotor arm. At this point a seemingly unconnected Sabini gang member standing by suggested that they take the Sabinis' Crossley truck. And they took his advice. And three miles down the road, near the Brick Kiln pub, the Brummagem man with the binoculars spotted the Sabini vehicle. 'Here they come, boys,' he said and his pals hiding in the lane readied themselves for battle.

And the Sabinis? Well, they had known what to expect. In any case, they had alternative transport and took another route home.

During the five-day trial Mr Travers Humphries led for the prosecution. Among the expensive line-up of defence barristers was Sir Ernest Wild QC. Much time was spent on identification. All of those in the dock insisted that they had not been involved with the affray. Some said that they had travelled on another bus

Darby Sabini.

to the rendezvous at the George and Dragon. Others claimed to have gone there to meet friends. Even the bus driver could not assure the court of the identity of his passengers. Although he had driven them to the races every day the party kept changing, he said. As a consequence of the problems of identification five men were acquitted. Of course, Billy Kimber and his lieutenants, Brown and Sage, never appeared before the court.

There were attempts to blacken the characters of the men who had been attacked. They were no shrinking violets. Hadn't Charlie Swartz been inside half a dozen times? Most of them were just as bad as the men who were responsible for the assault.

At the conclusion of the trial 22 of the original 28 accused were found guilty. John Lee, a 40 year old bookmaker who had a conviction for manslaughter and three other wounding charges, was given three years' imprisonment. Joseph Witton, another bookmaker, with many convictions, received a similar sentence. John Allard who had served seven years for manslaughter in 1912 – he had killed a man by jabbing the ferrule of an umbrella in his eye

– was sent down for 18 months. Three others received similar periods of imprisonment. Edward Banks who had shot at Darby Sabini in a fracas the previous year and who had suggested arming himself with Mills bombs was given 15 months. Others among the accused were sentenced to between 9 and 18 months. 'Cockney Bill' Graham, a pimp who had previously served five years for wounding and who now lived off his doxy's thefts from her clients, was among those who were acquitted. They were a remarkably unpleasant group.

On the Saturday evening, at the end of the trial, huge crowds gathered in Guildford High Street to witness the departure of the convicted men, who left in a bus singing snatches of popular songs.

'This sort of blackguardism in charabancs by numbers of ruffians descending on the country and committing outrages will be stamped out,' Mr Justice Rowlatt had observed when passing sentence. Of course he was wrong. What he described as 'blackguardism' lasted on this scale for another dozen years or so. Only months after the affair at Epsom, Darby Sabini shot and wounded Billy Kimber. True to the gangland code Kimber did not identify his assailant to the police.

And some years later, just like medieval barons, Darby Sabini and Billy Kimber reached an accord. The northern courses were to be within the Brummagem fiefdom. In the south it was the Sabinis who held sway.

But there were still battles ahead.

MYSTERY AT LOWER KNAPHILL

———————— ❖ ————————

It was that dead time, two o'clock in the morning, too late for night revellers and too early for anyone to be setting off for work. Woking, silent now, at rest, save up at St John's churchyard. For here, from inside and around the tarpaulin curtain that masked the unmarked grave, there were restrained voices, little more than whispers, and the occasional stifled laugh, the stamp and scuffle of chilled feet in the damp of the early March day and the clink and scrape of shovel and spade. And then it was brought up, the coffin that had lain in the earth for almost two years. Now it was the turn of the pathologist, Sir Bernard Spilsbury, to make what he could of the remains.

Examination revealed no sign of any injury. In the stomach there was no evidence of either disease or poisoning. Spilsbury noted: 'death not due to cerebral haemorrhage, and no other disease of the brain. Some senile changes, eg in arteries and kidneys. No disease to account for death or symptoms preceding it.' Hilary Rougier had been an old man, admittedly, but even so there was nothing that Spilsbury could find which could account for his death. But what about the conclusion of the local doctor, made at the time of death, that the causes were a cerebral haemorrhage and senile decay? No, Spilsbury could not accept that. Nor could he offer any other explanation for the old man's demise. At least not in any court.

Unsurprisingly Spilsbury had an idea of what might have happened. Why else would there have been a request to the Home Office for an exhumation? Something shady was suspected. In his notebook he indicates his view of events at Lower Knaphill.

'Before his death,' he writes, 'most of deceased's money had passed into hands of the Lerwills. Forged cheques?' But it's only conjecture that in some way the Lerwills had managed to fleece and then murder their long-time guest and friend. It was never proved. The matter never went as far as a criminal court. In fact, it never went beyond an inquest and there the matter rested, has rested, for nearly eighty years.

It's an odd case. There's no proof that Hilary Rougier was murdered. His family always maintained that he was and indeed there were the most suspicious circumstances. But that's not enough for the law.

In June 1926 the Lerwills, William and May, a young couple with two children, on the face of it eminently respectable, had rented a large, rather handsome house, Nuthurst, in Lower Knaphill, just outside Woking. With them had come a 77 year old bachelor, Hilary Rougier, who for the past three years had lived with them in Bexhill, Hassocks and Broadbridge Heath as a paying guest. He had been friendly for many years with William Lerwill's parents and had now become permanently attached to the household of their son. Rougier was a man of independent means who had farmed for seven or eight years near Reading after which he had retired to Guernsey – in his thirties, it seems – leading a life of leisure, spending his time in country pursuits, shooting and horse-riding. Now in his last days, he was inactive, just pottering in the garden or taking short strolls with his dog. Increasingly he became feeble, unable to eat, and his condition so alarmed the children's nurse, Marjorie Aldridge, that she was deeply worried about him.

The Lerwills and their guest were unknown to Dr Brewer when he was asked to come to Nuthurst for the first time on 23 July 1926. They had been in residence for only a month. At the inquest the doctor would recall how May Lerwill brought Rougier, a small man with a drooping moustache, into the house from the garden. She explained that Rougier's voice had been weak lately and that he was troubled with a cough. He suffered from asthma too. But Brewer found little wrong with his new patient. There were slight signs of bronchial trouble but nothing remarkable considering his advanced age. What Dr Brewer most noticed was that the old man seemed very subdued. And what irritated him was that he seemed never to answer the questions put to him. Instead, Mrs Lerwill constantly interrupted before he had the opportunity to utter more than one or two words. 'He answered my questions in monosyllables occasionally,' Dr Brewer was to tell the coroner, 'but as a rule Mrs Lerwill, vulgarly speaking, butted in before he had any chance to reply for himself. All information I sought to obtain from my patient direct was promptly given by Mrs Lerwill.'

And on the two subsequent visits that Dr Brewer paid to Nuthurst, Mrs Lerwill constantly spoke for Hilary Rougier. The old man did not volunteer any statement or make any remarks of his own. In the light of what emerged later some were to wonder if Rougier was somehow dominated by Mrs Lerwill. Or was he now just old and dependent?

When the doctor visited the house again on 28 July and 6 August Mrs Lerwill stated that the prescribed cough medicine had been quite effective and that her only concern now was that

Nuthurst. (Courtesy of Iain Wakeford)

Rougier was a little short of breath. Considering the man's age, perhaps Dr Brewer was little surprised by this.

Then on 24 August, a Saturday, at 8 o'clock in the morning, Mrs Lerwill telephoned the doctor. It was a matter of urgency, she said. Mr Rougier, she told him, was in a coma. When the housemaid had taken up his shaving water she could not waken him.

When Brewer arrived he found Rougier unconscious, his pulse weak, and his breathing shallow. He had been all right the previous day Mrs Lerwill said. He had not had much appetite but he had not complained of feeling unwell.

But nothing could be done for him, the doctor told her. He had suffered a severe cerebral haemorrhage in the night. It was just a matter of time now.

Several hours later Mrs Lerwill telephoned Dr Brewer. Rougier was dead. Of natural causes, the doctor said. And that is how matters stood until Sir Bernard Spilsbury, particularly dubious about the lack of any obvious medical causes and the period of unconsciousness preceding death, delivered his opinion nearly two years later.

Since Rougier's death there had been doubts within the family. It was really a matter of his will, drawn up in October 1919, and in which he had bequeathed 'all my property to my dearly beloved sister'. He had been expected to leave about £5,000 – at today's value £200,000. Instead there was a mere £79 (around £3,000). And that fact not unnaturally caused Rougier's sister, Mrs Ethel Carey-Smith, some concern.

Mrs Carey-Smith's daughter, Mrs Hilliard, telephoned Nuthurst from her home in Chigwell as soon as news of Rougier's death came through. When Mrs Lerwill expressed her wish to have the funeral as soon as possible, perhaps she did not attach much importance to it. Mrs Lerwill explained that her husband was away on business and that she was alone in the house with two small children. There was no objection to an early funeral from either Mrs Hilliard or from her mother. Certainly, make arrangements as soon as possible, she said. But would the family like to have a cremation, Mrs Lerwill asked. No, on no account, came the reply. Not a cremation. Mrs Carey-Smith detested the idea. But it was only in the days and weeks after the funeral that Mrs Hilliard and Mrs Carey-Smith began to wonder more deeply about Mrs Lerwill's proposed cremation.

Within days Hilary Rougier was buried at St John's church. Richard Hilliard, representing his mother-in-law, attended the funeral and afterwards went back to the house with the Lerwills. Mrs Carey-Smith, as executrix of her brother's will, had asked him to look out for certain personal belongings and the Lerwills helped him to search through the old man's effects. But the cheque book, where was that? It was nowhere to be found. Hilliard returned home, assuming that it would turn up somewhere in the house and that the Lerwills would send it on in the next few days.

But from then on matters became increasingly suspicious, at least as far as Mrs Carey-Smith and her solicitor, Arthur Crosse, were concerned. Crosse had drawn up Rougier's will in 1919 and he was bewildered to discover how little money there now was in the estate. Where had it all gone? Had the old man squandered it somehow? On the stock market? On some property investments? And how had he managed to pay the Lerwills for his keep if he had so little capital? What about his bank account in Guernsey? Perhaps it was lodged there. But no. That account had been closed. Nor was there any new account in any other bank.

The answer, Crosse was sure, lay at Lower Knaphill but when, a month after the funeral, he presented himself there he found Mrs Lerwill extremely unhelpful. She was unwilling to discuss any matters relating to Rougier's financial situation and referred him, rather resentfully, to her solicitor in Brighton. Odd, wasn't it, to treat the family's solicitor in this way? Downright suspicious, some might say.

Nor was the Lerwills' solicitor any more helpful. He was not going to discuss his clients' affairs with a stranger, even if he was a professional colleague.

And then Crosse discovered Hilary Rougier's bank passbook though where he came upon it is unclear. Perhaps it was among the effects that Richard Hilliard had brought from Nuthurst. And it was a most astonishing document. Over a two year period from 1924 until the year of Rougier's death in 1926 a considerable number of cheques had been made out to both Lerwills. One cheque for £130 went into William Lerwill's account. Then there were other substantial sums made out in favour of May Lerwill – one for £60, another £50, yet another for £120. On 15 January 1925 a cheque for £1,850 from Rougier was paid into Mrs Lerwill's account in a Horsham bank, purportedly signed by him but made out, Mrs Carey-Smith was sure, by another hand.

Throughout this period Hilary Rougier had been living with the Lerwills. He was of sound mind. Presumably he was aware of what he was doing. Was he the type of man to throw his money around? Not in the opinion of his sister. And she was quite certain that the cheques had not been written by him. Not his handwriting, she said. Definitely not.

And then there was the house in Guernsey, which over the years Rougier had rented out. It had always been Mrs Carey-Smith's expectation that this property would eventually pass to her. In the spring of 1925, when she last saw her brother at Broadbridge Heath, talk had turned to the Guernsey property. She was quite convinced that it was still her brother's intention that she should inherit the house. But now she recalled an incident that at the time she had perhaps little regarded. During the conversation Mrs Lerwill asked to speak to Rougier privately. Now Mrs Carey-Smith had discovered that the house had been sold for £3,080, money which no doubt had gone into Rougier's ever-dwindling accounts.

And so it was this factor – the suspicion by members of his family that Hilary Rougier had been defrauded – that led to the exhumation at Woking in March 1928 and to Sir Bernard Spilsbury's rejection of Dr Brewer's diagnosis that death was due to natural causes.

The inquest was held at Woking in May 1928. There were two strands that required clarification. There was a need to account for what had really happened to Rougier's money and how, if not from natural causes, he had died.

At the inquest Spilsbury presented his findings and after him came the Home Office analyst, Dr Roche Lynch, who described the discovery of faint traces of morphine in the organs. But, as Lynch explained, this was not the total amount taken. Poison disappears as a body putrefies and what was surprising to him was the presence of morphine so long after death. This suggested that significantly more had been ingested very shortly before Rougier died. Furthermore those poisoned with morphine become drowsy and then fall into a coma. Their pulse slows down and, over a period of between six and twelve hours, death follows. This was precisely how Dr Brewer found Rougier on the day of his death.

Then was it a case of morphine poisoning? the jury foreman asked.

'I have not said that in so many words,' Lynch answered, surprisingly cautiously. He had deduced that a considerable quantity of morphine had been taken, that it was possibly a fatal dose, but he would go no further.

Lynch also said that the police had handed over to him 119 items of drugs, food preparations and medicines found at Nuthurst. One bottle of cough medicine labelled 'Linctus – to be taken if the cough is troublesome' contained 0.15 per cent morphine. A bottle of laudanum contained one per cent morphine. Even a small amount of this had been known to cause death and certainly a full bottle would have constituted, if not a fatal dose, certainly, in the analyst's words, 'getting on towards it'.

Dr Roche Lynch's contribution to the inquest must undoubtedly have left the jury with the idea that Hilary Rougier had been poisoned. When he was questioned Dr Brewer accepted that he had been mistaken and that a cerebral haemorrhage had not caused the old man's death.

More in this vein was to come with the arrival before the court of Miss Mary Hope who in June 1926 had rented Nuthurst to the Lerwills for the 'considerable sum' of four and a half guineas per week. She had locked up some cupboards in the house including one which had for the past twenty years or so contained about 120 bottles, some of which had contained poisons. They had belonged to her late father, a doctor. The lock to this cupboard, Miss Hope said, was faulty and it was possible for anyone to open it. When she left the house the laudanum bottle, she was sure, had contained about two divisions more than there were when she returned in October 1926. There was, however, and not unreasonably, some doubt cast on her ability to recall this with such precision.

Miss Lilian Hope, sister of the previous witness, told the court that the Lerwills had arranged to pay the rent of the house in instalments. The first instalment had been paid but a cheque received for the second had been returned from Barclays bank marked 'Return to drawer'. The matter, Miss Hope now said, was in the hands of the family solicitor.

The Lerwills unable to pay the rent? Well, in 1925, when living at Broadbridge Heath, they had been unable to pay their water bill and there were threats to cut off the supply. Rougier had come to the rescue. So how were they now managing to pay for their children's nurse and the maid? Had they been so desperate for cash that they had swindled Hilary Rougier? And then when his money had almost run out ... what then? But they all seemed to be so fond of each other. Rougier had told his sister that he regarded William as his son and the nurse, Marjorie Aldridge, said how attached he was to the Lerwills. Mrs Carey-Smith admitted in court that her brother had written to her only a fortnight before his death to say how happy he was.

Then it was the turn of William Lerwill to answer to the court. He had, he said, no present occupation although he was looking for employment. He was now living at Chesham and his wife with her parents at Bexhill – for financial reasons, he explained. Later he spoke about a catering business in Woking that had failed. Had it not done so he would have had no difficulty in paying the rent. Lerwill also mentioned a failed training stable that Rougier had again tried to bale out but all too late. In the course of his evidence it was abundantly clear that Lerwill rarely succeeded at anything in business. How then had he managed to live over the years in some style? All that was thanks to Hilary Rougier, he answered. For many years, and long before he lived with the Lerwills, the old man had helped with certain business arrangements, sometimes with money and sometimes with shares. 'Certain business arrangements' was a euphemism, Lerwill's language for 'constant pressing debts'.

Lerwill maintained that the cheques were always signed by Rougier even if he or his wife wrote them out. No, he said, Rougier never paid rent or anything for his board. But instead, from time to time, he paid out various sums of money.

What about a cheque for £80 made out to Mrs Lerwill, he was asked. What about other cheques? What about the cheque for £1,850: how was that to be explained? They were all for the same purpose, said Lerwill. They were to pay off debt after debt after debt. 'He wanted to help me and he did,' Lerwill told the court. 'He said he had never been so happy in his life as when he was living with me.'

But what if Rougier's money ran out? What then? From what he told the court Lerwill appeared never to have given this any thought. He claimed not to know how much Rougier had in his bank. He had just assumed he would always have enough money. Was William Lerwill so feckless and so unintelligent? Had he really given no consideration to Rougier's financial affairs? Here was a man, a complete failure in financial terms, borrowing money at every turn from his old friend. It had been going on for years. Yet he claimed that he had never wondered if Rougier could afford the constant paying out. This man's whole world was about money and pressing debt. Did he never think of putting the question – how long could he keep on coming to the well? Did he have a hold over the old man? Did he threaten him? Was this how he got so much money out of Rougier? Had Dr Brewer seen an old man intimidated by Mrs Lerwill?

But just supposing the old man's money did run out. How then would he have maintained himself, Lerwill was asked.

'I have not the faintest idea. I should have looked after him or my people would.'

Would they? Why should they?

But Lerwill was airily assured on this. 'My people would have looked after him if I asked them.'

And what about the week before Rougier died: where was Lerwill then? In Brighton, he said, in Colchester and then in London.

Doing what? Alas, the question was not put. Was it some other hopeless business venture, some other scheme destined to fail? Was that it? The record is silent on this. But he did return to the house on the day that Rougier took ill. His wife had telephoned him and he had returned post-haste, he said. But he had stayed at Nuthurst for only a couple of hours. Was this hurried visit, as his wife was to suggest, to support his old friend in his last hours? Or was there some other purpose?

And apropos the morphine found in the body. Could he say anything about that?

No, he could say nothing about any poison.

'Do you suggest he got it by himself?' the coroner asked.

'He might have done,' came the answer.

'Do you consider he took it himself?'

'I cannot say.'

And the laudanum he purchased for Mr Rougier's dog's claws, what about that? Yes, Lerwill said, he had bought laudanum and recalled having signed a chemist's register for it. But where – perhaps Woking or Horsham, he fancied – he was unsure. It was a poor performance and William Lerwill seems to have come over unconvincingly. But he was not on trial. The purpose of the inquest was simply to establish the cause of death.

Mrs Lerwill's responses were no more reassuring than her husband's. Take for example this reply to a question: 'I did not know what my husband's income was but I knew that a friend was helping him. It was not until Mr Crosse called at Nuthurst that I knew that the friend was Mr Rougier.'

In December 1925, because of her husband's impending bankruptcy, May Lerwill had opened an account at Barclays bank in Horsham and it was there that she paid in several cheques, signed so it seems, by Hilary Rougier. One of these cheques was for £1,850.

But like her husband she knew nothing of Rougier's financial situation, had no idea that his money was almost exhausted.

As for any poison, she had never bought any, was unaware of her husband's buying any, nor had she seen any in a cupboard at Nuthurst.

It was all decidedly fishy.

In his summing up the coroner advised the jury that they should not name anyone in a verdict involving a criminal offence unless they were satisfied beyond all reasonable doubt that there was sufficient evidence to support a further criminal charge.

After half an hour the jury returned a verdict that Hilary Rougier had died of morphine poisoning – **not self-administered.**

No names but enough to indicate that the jury was convinced that the old man had been murdered.

But nothing then happened. The Lerwills were not charged with any offence, presumably because the evidence was purely circumstantial. Rougier's sister did not pursue them for any money for typically they had none. But later William sued a couple of newspapers for libel out of which he made £5,000 and he subsequently deserted his wife and children and went to Canada.

Then, in March 1934, Lerwill briefly made another headline. He had returned to England where he littered the land with a trail of dud cheques. At Combe Martin in Devon, he was approached in the street by a police constable who challenged him about an unpaid hotel bill. Out of his pocket he took a small phial of prussic acid. Presumably the game was up. Time to stop running. Life was all too complex. There in the street he swallowed the acid.

So back to the main point. Was Hilary Rougier murdered by the young couple he so loved and whom he so regularly and willingly helped? Could they have done it? Did William, coming back from London that Friday afternoon for only two hours, do the deed? Or was the old man being progressively poisoned, perhaps by Mrs Lerwill, ever since their arrival at Nuthurst. Could they have been so wicked? Did they commit that worst of crimes – the betrayal of trust? Perhaps …

LORDS OF THE EARTH

———————————❁———————————

L ook at them. Say you knew nothing about them. Say you just
saw their photographs and nothing more, no detail, no
background. Or say you passed them in the street, just had a
glimpse of them. What would you make of them? Have another
look. There's not a line, not a furrow on the brow, not a sag in the
jaw. They're clear eyed, smooth skinned, fresh. They're at the start
of things. For them there are years ahead. And you can see they're
fine looking boys. Maybe they're students. They look responsible
types, the sort of young men you know are going to turn out well.
Get their qualifications, become reliable employees, meet nice girls
and marry and have wonderful children, reach positions of trust
and responsibility. That's how they look. That's the kind of idea
you get at first sight. Their decency seems to shine through. Good
boys, good young men. That's what they are, what they look like.
And that's what they should be because they're from decent,
respectable families.

But things haven't turned out that way and you wonder why.
And you look at their homes and there's not a breath of suspicion
there. You can play the psychologist and point the finger at their
families but there's nothing that gives a clue as to why they acted
as they did. And the madness of it is that they had such good
prospects, all three of them. And they've thrown it away. They've
been called 'thrill seekers' and that may be part of the truth, a
group of boys – it's almost unfair to call them men – out for
excitement. But they are described more harshly too. They have
been called 'flashy thugs' and 'monsters'. Can you believe it when
you look at their pictures? But you must be the judge of that.

Matthew Dove, a 20 year old from Addlestone, was a potential
world motocross champion. He already had a £50,000

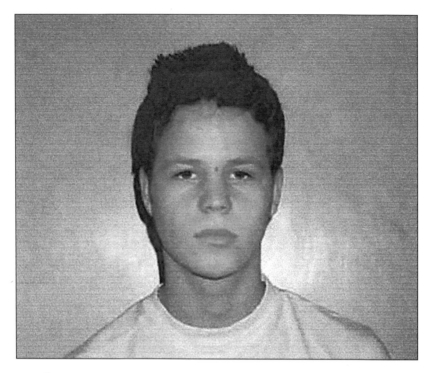

Matthew Dove (courtesy of Surrey Police).

sponsorship deal. Five years on and he might have been a millionaire. His friend Gareth Davies, 21, from Ashford had impressed motorcycle clothing manufacturers so much that he had a contract with them. Thomas Chesterman, 18 years old, who came from Reading was already regarded as a future top rider. They were there, ready, poised to take the motocross world by storm. They were ace riders, skilful, stylish, daring and tough, taking their 500cc bikes round rough circuits, over jumps and other obstacles. And among the followers of the sport they had countless admirers. And there is nothing like admiration, adoration, for making anyone, let alone young men, feel on top of the world, like young princes, with a golden future rolling out in front of them.

Gareth Davies (courtesy of Surrey Police).

They were all close friends, training together on racetracks, exercising in gyms and clubbing. And spending. Jewellery, champagne, good restaurants. Motocross riders? You wouldn't have thought that if you had seen them off track, if you'd seen them about town. You'd have thought they were members of some boy band, Westlife maybe, with their designer clothes, their bleached blond hair, their style, their swagger. Arrogant, perhaps, but then they were successful. They tasted success every time they went on the track. And there was always the back-slapping, the congratulations, the girls reaching forward to touch them. How could they think of themselves as other than lords of the earth? Heady stuff, fame and celebrity. Forget the fact that most of us had never heard of them, that we knew little enough of their sport. In their world they were up at the top.

But the buzz was not enough. They could not get sufficient thrills from the jerky risks of motocross. There must be

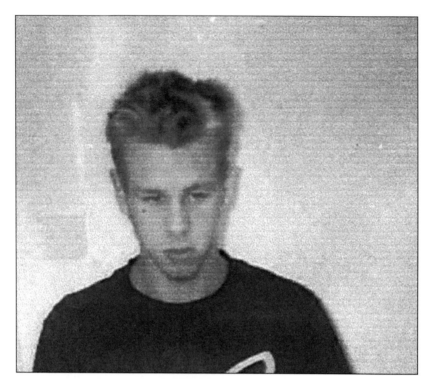

Thomas Chesterman (courtesy of Surrey Police).

something else, though who thought of the alternative sport – if that is how they viewed it – is not known. Perhaps it was some champagne-guzzling evening when they thought it up. Just musing about some film perhaps, how a character got away with murder or if not murder, then with the proceeds of some heist or other. And perhaps someone said that they could do that. Nothing to stop them doing something of that kind. Pull off a robbery. And perhaps the others did not believe him, scoffed at him. But maybe he persisted and in the end they were convinced. Yes, maybe he was right. Maybe they could pull something off. And so they tried it out. Just for the buzz really, so they told themselves.

So it began, an eight week rampage. On 4 December 2001 two masked men went into the Wendover Stores in Egham. They threatened the shopkeeper and made off with the till. They made their getaway in a car. Four days later it was the Hythe End Stores in Wraysbury and on 13 December the Londis Store in Stanwell. On 15 December they attacked Ruby Wines at Englefield Green and the next day they were at the Village Stores at Burghfield Common.

But it was the style they adopted that alerted police. These were all small stores, usually with no more than three or four staff and not the kinds of places accustomed to being robbed. And certainly not by masked men armed with sub-machine guns and revolvers and knives. And not by men wearing balaclavas or 'Scream' or Elvis masks, men who charged in suddenly just before closing time, screaming and threatening customers and staff, kicking and pushing them to the ground. One proprietor was slashed across the face by a knife waved in front of him and then the raiders rammed the till into his wife's stomach sending her sprawling. A gun was held to the head of another shopkeeper. 'Give me the money or I'll kill you,' his assailant told him. And it was over in a couple of minutes at most, the robbers running out with the till to their waiting car.

On 19 December a female driver was targeted on the M25 and followed by the robbers until she stopped at the Weybridge Trading Estate in Addlestone. She was dragged from her £26,000 Subaru Impreza by her hair. On the same evening, using the stolen vehicle as a getaway car, they robbed Unwins at Harmanswater, Bracknell.

In only three weeks the gang had earned a reputation for excessive force. They had terrified shopkeepers and shoppers unnecessarily. They seemed to be enjoying that aspect of their activity.

On 22 December the gang robbed Thamesside Stores at Weybridge and on New Year's Eve Dillons in Sudbury.

At the BP garage car wash in Staines on 6 January 2002 a woman drying her car was roughly bundled aside and fell to the ground. Two men in balaclavas drove off in her Audi A3 worth £30,000. Some time later the car was found by police with false number plates, S3BAD. The fingerprints of one of the thieves – Dove – were found on the inside but there was no indication of whose they were in police records.

At the post office in Englefield Green on 9 January the manager was injured when he was manhandled by the gang and there were further robberies at Budgens in Sunbury on 30 January and at the Shepperton Superstore on 3 February.

So much activity suggests a confidence that they would not be caught. For the men did not need the money they stole. They had accumulated about £11,000 in eight weeks and of course nearly £100,000 worth of stolen cars although these were usually abandoned after being used in raids. Surely their luck could not hold out, for it does seem that they were determined just to go on and on and on. Perhaps they enjoyed not just the thrill of their activities. Perhaps they were enjoying too much the power they could exert over lone women in cars, the force they could exert over their frightened victims.

On 5 February Matthew Dove went to the exclusive Foxhills Golf and Country Club in Weybridge. He had followed the driver of a Cherokee Jeep 4 x 4 to the clubhouse where he had managed to steal the car keys from his jacket pocket.

Later in the evening an off-duty policeman noticed two young men acting suspiciously at a garage in Old Windsor. It was Dove and Chesterman and it is likely that they were on the look-out for lone women drivers. When they were approached the men drove off in the Cherokee and a police alarm was sent out. There followed a reckless chase at high speeds and full of high performance stunts. Twice Dove reversed into the pursuing police car. Other cars were crashed into and at one point, trying to escape, the Cherokee was driven over the top of another vehicle. Seen on American films it looks so staged; seen on video games it looks so easy. But this is how the Cherokee was driven for over eight miles that evening. Until at last in Westwood Road, Windlesham, the car came to a halt. The chase was finished and the vehicle abandoned. The car's occupants fled into the dark. But a police dog found Chesterman hiding in some bushes. It was now all but over for the gang.

In the Cherokee was a holdall containing an imitation Uzi sub-machine gun, an imitation handgun, a knife, a hammer, an Elvis mask, a 'Scream' mask and two balaclavas.

The homes of the other gang members were searched shortly afterwards and items belonging to the victims of the car-jackings – women's swimwear, sunglasses, the keys to one of the cars –

were found. Police later discovered pairs of distinctive multi-coloured motocross gloves, which the robbers had worn on raids. These were to provide vital evidence at their six-week trial. What also became obvious during the police investigation was that not all of the gang had been caught.

In July 2003 five men appeared at Guildford Crown Court charged with conspiracy to rob. Two were acquitted but Dove, Davies and Chesterman were found guilty.

Sentencing the three, Judge Keith Bassingthwaighte commented, 'Targeting vulnerable people in small shops is something the courts will always deal with severely. The sentence may serve as a deterrent to others who prey upon vulnerable people in the community with such heartless and selfish arrogance.'

The three young men were sentenced to nine years' imprisonment. Dove was sentenced to a further 18 months for the theft of the Cherokee, this sentence to run concurrently with his nine-year jail term. But the men appeared not to have been chastened by their experience. When sentence was handed down they kicked at the dock and swore. After all they had believed themselves untouchable, thought themselves lords of the earth. They were going right to the top of their exciting profession. They were to be champions, constantly in the public eye, admired. They thought they could do anything.

But not everyone has such an admiration for the so-called 'designer robbers'. Perhaps the comment of one of the defence counsel hurt them as much as anything that was said about them. 'They were hardly Al Capone,' he commented. 'More like Westlife with a hangover.' That must sting the amour-propre of the lords of the earth.

And Detective Constable Anthony Archibald of the Surrey Police Serious Crime Team had little sympathy for them. He had to deal with their terrified victims. 'These young men had promising careers in motocross,' he said, 'but they displayed violence to their victims and put them through a frightening experience … Crimes like this will not be tolerated. We are delighted they have been given such a considerable time behind bars.'

But in the end one can only reflect on the waste, everything thrown away. For nothing but cheap thrills and the exercise of a temporary brutal power over total strangers.

THE GREAT CROYDON AIRPORT GOLD BULLION ROBBERY

❋

Odd how things turn out. What has been described as a very cleverly planned and well executed crime nearly crumbled to dust because of an alert cyclist and a sharp-eyed landlady. As a result the police were able to make arrests within days. But, they never recovered the gold valued at £214,000 and worth, at today's estimate, more than £11,250,000.

And it was all stolen from Britain's major airport – Croydon. And don't be surprised at that. After all, as the *Wallington and Carshalton Times* boasted in May 1935: 'The fame of Croydon Airport is world-wide ... It has become a gateway to the Empire.' Croydon Airport was a byword for style. A trip to the Continent? No need to take the Dover-Calais boat train now. Go Imperial Airways. Just travel down to Croydon and fly over. The romance of it, the style of it. It was now the done thing for bright young things to take a flip from Croydon to Paris or Berlin or Prague. Rather like hopping over to Bali or the Seychelles today for a long weekend.

And they flew freight from here. And mail too. And gold bullion.

Think gold, think security.

Unfortunately security, 1935-style, was not as effective as it is today.

Croydon Airport was on Purley Way, on the west side of the town. Two main entrance gates, open day and night, led to the main building and to the car park. Don't imagine it contained shopping malls, extensive customs halls, carpeted lounges. It was a much smaller enterprise than anything like today's Gatwicks and Heathrows. In the main building, only 100 yards from the entrance where the police office and a gate-keeper's hut were located, were the ticket desks, offices and a modest restaurant. And the strongroom. This main building was not locked nor was there anyone on duty at the doors. Imperial Airways had only one man on duty on the night of the theft. Allegedly there were also two Air Ministry men present though what precisely their duties amounted to was never stated. At 10.30 pm on the night after the robbery, a *Daily Express* reporter strolled into the buildings. He later wrote that the gate-keeper's hut was unoccupied and the main entrance unattended. He wandered around unchallenged for half an hour.

The Great Croydon Airport Gold Bullion Robbery had been just waiting to happen. When at 7 o'clock on the morning of 6 March 1935 Francis Johnson, the import clerk, the man who had been on duty all night, went to the strongroom, he found its outer wooden door locked but the inner steel door unlocked. Worse, three boxes of gold, shut inside the previous evening, had vanished.

When officers from Scotland Yard arrived they must have been astounded to learn of the arrangements, which were lax in the extreme, and the sheer complacency of those responsible for the haphazard manner in which such valuable cargo was managed. Even later in the magistrates' court and at the subsequent trial the self-assurance of those allegedly in charge was astonishing.

Three boxes of gold had been collected by van on the afternoon of 5 March from the Westminster bank at Lothbury. The van was never left unattended and its doors were locked the whole time except for the few seconds when it was being loaded. The boxes were to be taken to Croydon and then, by early morning flights, one was to be sent on to Brussels and two to Paris.

George Auguste, the export clerk, and Samuel Roberts, a loader, received the gold at the airport at about seven in the evening. After weighing, the boxes were taken to the export shed – which was not locked – and there they remained in full view for the next three hours. Asked at the trial if he thought it wise to leave over £200,000 worth of gold in boxes for three hours in an open shed, Roberts replied, 'It is not for me to say.' The gold was within his sight and that of two trainees working there the whole time, he said. That arrangement seemed to be good enough for Roberts and for his superiors. Herbert Higgins, Imperial Airways' station superintendent, seemed only to know after the event, when he turned up for work the following morning, that the gold had been in the export shed for three hours. Pressed on this matter at the trial, he was asked if he did not think it unwise to leave the gold in the export shed for so long before it was transferred to the strongroom. 'I don't think it unwise,' he answered.

Higgins was on duty until 9.20 pm on 5 March. How could he not be aware of the whereabouts of such a valuable cargo? When he left he locked the keys of the strongroom in his desk and took home the desk key. A duplicate set of strongroom keys was in the possession of Auguste, who was working late.

An hour later Auguste and Roberts carried the three boxes from the export shed into the strongroom. Auguste locked both the inner steel door and the outer wooden door and handed over the keys to Francis Johnson when he left at midnight.

Now only Johnson was on duty in the airport's main building. At about 12.30 am, in accordance with usual practice, he locked himself in the import office and went to sleep. He had the keys to the strongroom in his pocket. At 4.15 am his alarm clock awakened him and he went out to the flying ground to receive a German airliner due at 4.30 am. Before leaving he locked the door of the import office. When he returned at about 5 o'clock the door was still locked.

Johnson was still the only member of staff on the premises until 6 o'clock. And then at 7 o'clock he and another clerk went to the strongroom and found it empty. The three boxes, containing three bars of gold, 5,000 United States gold coins and 5,800 sovereigns, had disappeared.

The laxness that pervaded the operation of security is undeniable. Even so, how had the robbers managed to get into and out of the airport? How had they had the freedom to walk into the strongroom? Higgins had left a set of strongroom keys in his locked desk and yet the desk was not broken into. The keys were still in the drawer. And first Auguste and then Johnson had had the sole keeping of the duplicate set and had kept it in their pockets. It was evident that someone had another set of keys.

So keys and timing, that was what the police were working on in the first hours. Was it an inside job? Who had spirited the boxes away? And when? Presumably, they went during the time that Johnson was attending to the German aircraft.

But solving a mystery is often down to luck. And within hours Alfred King turned up to speak to the police. He had been cycling to work shortly after 5 o'clock that morning and about a mile from the airport he saw a small car followed by a taxicab. Of course, today we assume that there will be motorcars on the roads at all hours. Not so in 1935. King, who probably had never ridden in a car, let alone owned one, was intrigued. It seemed obvious to him that the two vehicles were together. This struck him as so odd that when he heard about the robbery, he reported what he had seen to the police. Anything else? Oh yes, he said, there was something else. He'd taken the number of the taxi.

It was not difficult to trace George Manson, the taxi driver. He lived in Hornsey. And he was in no position to deny that his taxi had been seen in the vicinity of the airport in the early hours of Tuesday morning. He'd been on a job, he told the police.

He'd had a fare. One o'clock in the morning, and a chap had come hammering at his door and got him out of bed. Would he come along to King's Cross station at 4 o'clock? Do a bit of driving? It's a feller he knows as Little Harry. Anyway, George turns up at King's Cross at the appointed hour and there's Little Harry and three others. Off they go down through Thornton Heath, through Croydon and onto Purley Way. And here, three quarters of a mile from the airport, all four passengers get out of the car and set off on foot in the direction of the airport. George is told to wait. It's about a quarter to five now. They won't be long, they tell him.

Then after twenty minutes or so a small, rather dilapidated black car comes along from the direction of the airport and stops near George's taxi. Four men get out and then they're putting three boxes in the taxi and George hears the word 'gold'. Well, he thinks there's something wrong here but although he protests the men go on arranging the boxes in the back of his taxi and then three of the men climb in. The fourth man drives off in the small car and George follows him.

Mrs Swanland (Daily Mail, 1935).

They drive all the way to Harringay, to Pemberton Road, and they get there about 6.30 am. They call at a house and a young woman answers the door and then Little Harry and another man carry the boxes into the house.

Armed with this information Detective Inspector Widdocks went to the house in Pemberton Road to search the rooms occupied by Cecil Swanland and his wife. When Swanland, 47 years old and described as an artist, was told that it was suspected that stolen gold had been brought to the house, he dismissed the idea as being outrageous. 'Perfectly ridiculous,' he said. 'I have been reading about it during the day. If you think there is any gold here you are quite at liberty to search.'

And there on the table was the newspaper, open at the page containing a report of the theft. A number of pencil marks suggested that somebody had been studying it closely. Also on the table was an Imperial Airways timetable. It was enough to encourage the detectives to think that they were looking in the right area.

Their subsequent search of the fireplace turned up other items of interest. There had been a considerable fire in the grate. Among the ashes were a number of nails and an iron band similar to those used to secure the boxes of bullion. And in a dustbin were several seals bearing the name 'Messrs Japhet and Co'. One of the missing bullion boxes had been consigned by Japhets.

And most significant, in a jacket belonging to Swanland, there was a long wire key, 'not the sort any ordinary person would have in his possession', Detective Inspector Widdocks was to say later. 'It is a long, narrow wire key and one which would only be in the possession of a person requiring keys for an extraordinary purpose. The key fits the lock of the inner door of the strongroom. Although it fits the lock and turns the lever it does not completely open it – at least at any rate, not in the hands of the police.'

But a clever operator, a man who knew his keys, would know how to make it work.

Unsurprisingly, Swanland was arrested and charged with the theft of the gold.

And Swanland's landlady, Mrs Schultz, was able to offer further interesting information to the police. On the morning of the robbery, at about 6.30, she saw a car drive up in front of the gate to the house. Swanland was there with another man. She saw Swanland reach into the car and take out something which he then carried into the house. She described him as rushing along the path and into the house.

Minutes later she heard a loud banging from Swanland's room. It was as though something was being forced and noises of bumping and door banging continued for several minutes. Then came the sounds of the fire being raked. Half an hour or so after that Mrs Schultz heard a window being opened and great billows of smoke passed over her window. Finally, she saw Swanland saying goodbye to another man and Mrs Schultz's early morning excitement came to an end.

But seemingly ever alert, she had seen her lodger that evening at about 7 o'clock standing at the gate as if waiting for someone. When a car arrived at the house she saw him go inside and then come out, carrying a large and obviously very heavy suitcase, which he put in the car.

Mrs Schultz's observations would be helpful in court.

In the next two days, and after a line-up at which they were identified by Manson, the taxi driver, two other men were arrested. One was John O'Brien, then in his mid-seventies, and the other a 38 year old bookmaker, Silvio Mazzarda.

Swanland was a raffish sort of man. In the magistrates' court, in which he appeared to take little interest in proceedings, he is described as wearing a smartly cut, dark blue, pinstripe suit, with a multi-coloured muffler round his neck and a silk spotted handkerchief in his breast pocket. Sufficient to say that when O'Brien and Mazzarda were arrested – both on different days – they chose not to wait for the arrival of police cars but instead hired taxis. They too were men of some style.

In the court Mr Graham Brooks for the prosecution referred to the robbery as a story 'as dramatic as any by Edgar Wallace'. And so it was. The court heard all about the discovery of the theft at the airport; about the early morning drive to Purley Way; about the house in Pemberton Road; about a witness, Mrs Schultz, being approached in the street by a man who threatened her with the words, 'Take my advice and keep your mouth shut.' They heard too that there was a fourth man, Little Harry, who was still being sought. 'This man is not yet in the dock,' Mr Brooks told the bench, 'and I can say nothing about him except to say that, as a result of what Little Harry said, Manson got up and dressed, took out a taxicab and turned up at King's Cross at 4 am.'

Mazzarda, the prosecution claimed, had driven the little black car from the airport car park, where it had been waiting all day, while the other three were driven back to Pemberton Road.

But there was a setback to the prosecution case when Manson claimed now not to recognise any of the men in the dock as his passengers on the night of the robbery. For the past thirty years, he said, he had known Mazzarda: he'd known him as 'Shonk', a nickname derived from his prominent nose. But Manson now swore that he had not seen him in the last five years.

As for O'Brien, a man he had never previously seen, he had been mistaken.

No, Manson said, no one had spoken to him about the evidence he was to give. No, he had not been threatened. But his statement

George Manson, taxi driver.

Mrs Schultz, Mrs Swanland's landlady.

to the police? His identification of O'Brien and Mazzarda at the identity parade? All a mistake, said Manson.

Small wonder that Brooks commented to the bench: 'Having heard that this witness refused to identify anybody and having observed his demeanour, I submit there is that in his conduct which entitles me to treat him as a hostile witness and to put to him questions on his signed statement.'

Under fierce questioning about his statement and the line-up Manson's answers were at least consistent. He came out with responses such as: 'I don't quite remember', 'I don't remember saying that', 'I really don't remember what I did say', 'I can't remember whether I did say it', 'I can't remember that', 'I said it was very doubtful', 'I can't say for certain', 'I was not quite sure it was him'.

Manson could not recall saying in his statement that it was Mazzarda who drove the small car up to his cab. He claimed to have told the officer at the identity parade that he was 'very doubtful about the old gentleman'.

Even so, in spite of the disappointment of Manson's testimony, the three men, charged with the theft of gold and receiving, went to trial before the Recorder of Croydon on 24 April 1935.

On the first day of the trial Mr Brooks mentioned a conversation that allegedly took place between a prisoner called Steele and Swanland while both were on remand at Brixton. Having read about the bullion robbery Steele said to Swanland, 'That's a smart job you pulled off at Croydon.' 'Yes,' Swanland had replied, 'but somebody's double-crossed us and they've found some seals.' 'Why worry if you have the stuff?' Steele had said, to which Swanland had answered, 'Oh yes, I have got that well planted. They will never get that.'

But prison officers denied that Steele ever spoke to Swanland and the Recorder dismissed the story.

Manson, true to form, continued to dispute his statement, claiming confusion and faulty memory. He now denied that Swanland was in his cab on the night of the robbery. Cross-examined on his statement he admitted that what he had told the police was not all true but at the time he had, he said, been muddled. True, he had said in his statement that he had no doubt

John O'Brien.

O'Brien was one of the men he drove to Purley Way, but now he did have doubts. And he agreed with the defence that he had told the police that the elderly man who had got into the cab was clean-shaven. But there was O'Brien, plain for all to see, with a moustache.

The Recorder told the jury that as the taxi driver's evidence against O'Brien was so unsure he did not think it would be safe to convict. After a brief consideration O'Brien was found not guilty and discharged.

As for the identification of 'Shonk' Mazzarda, Manson now said that the police had shown him a photograph of the man they wanted him to point out before the identity parade took place. Inspector Gorman had given instructions to him, saying, 'I want you to identify the man you know as Shonk.' The inspector denied this accusation.

For the prosecution Mr Brooks introduced a conversation a few days after the robbery when Detective Sergeant Cory talked to Mazzarda in a public house at Harlesden. Mazzarda was agitated and asked the policeman, 'Do you know if the man they have got for the gold job has "come it"?' He went on to ask, 'If he does and mentions other people, is that evidence against them?'

But this story was not enough to persuade the Recorder. And with Manson again stoutly denying that Mazzarda was in his taxi on the night of the robbery he confided his doubts about the case against the accused. As on the previous day the jury was told of the very grave dispute with regard to the identification of Mazzarda. There was no real evidence against the accused, the Recorder told the jury, and what there was came from a discredited source. In consequence the charges against Mazzarda were also dismissed.

For the defence Mr J.F. Eastwood, M.P. said there was evidence which undoubtedly placed Swanland under suspicion but no more than the two men who had been acquitted. The real charge against Swanland, Eastwood said, was the alternative one of receiving, probably knowing it to have been stolen. But he was innocent even of that, his counsel claimed.

Swanland told the court that he never saw any gold, that when he saw the boxes they were empty, that he had no idea that they had been stolen. He explained that on the morning of 6 March he went out for a walk round the park as he frequently did. That morning he saw a dog-racing acquaintance in a taxicab, a man he knew as 'Harry'. They had stopped to talk.

'He told me that he'd been out at a club binge,' Swanland said. 'Up against the seat of the cab and partly covered by a raincoat were three boxes. They were sticking out with nails and were open. The lids were in pieces and were sticking out at the top. I asked him what they were.' Harry had apparently answered, 'Some of the mob put them in and said, "There's your luggage."' It had been a typical practical joke, a raucous fooling around after a night on the tiles. That's what Swanland had thought.

Swanland said that when Harry told him he fancied a drink he invited him into his house. 'Little Harry didn't offer me the boxes,' Swanland said. 'I asked him for them. I took two of them in and he took in the other. Little Harry came into the house and had two drinks. The fire was alight but very poor.' The morning was cold and so they broke up the boxes that he had asked Harry to give him. 'I put some of the wood on and it made a lot of smoke.'

That evening Swanland said he had met a friend who brought his car round to the house and he went out with him. This was the occasion when Mrs Schultz saw him go out of the house. But according to Swanland he did not have a heavy case with him. He carried nothing but a walking stick.

Swanland was asked about his means. 'How much do you earn as a black and white artist?' Brooks enquired.

'A few pounds a week sometimes but things have been slack lately.'

'Did you on the day of the robbery receive payment for your work?'

'No.'

'The day after?'

'No.'

'Did you receive any payment during the week before this?'

'No.'

'Were you expecting a big payment for your work during the week prior to your arrest?'

'No.'

'Then why did you order £59 worth of clothes?'

'I was expecting commission from another kind of work.'

'Did you buy a pair of gold cuff links for £11 10 shillings?'

'Yes. I exchanged another pair on which I was allowed £5.'

'Where did you get the money for that?'

'On commission, working for bookmakers, and assisting my mother-in-law.'

'Did you select a brooch valued at £50 for your wife?'

'I admired one but did not select it.'

Where did Swanland, a poorly paid artist, earn enough to pay for such snappy clothing for himself and for such elegant apparel for his young wife in the week prior to the robbery?

Mrs Swanland, smartly dressed, only 21 years of age, and married for less than a year, said that on the night of 5 March her husband had gone to bed before midnight. She heard him go out the next morning at his usual time and she went to sleep again. She woke at 7.30 and when she went into the dining room noticed that some glasses had been used but she did not see or hear any visitor. Her complaint about police treatment, that she had been called 'a worse liar than her husband', availed her nothing.

In the end Cecil Swanland, described by the Recorder as 'a very dangerous man against whom society has got to be protected', was sentenced to seven years. Swanland was no blameless, misguided artist. He had variously described himself down the years as artist, journalist, engineer, financier and variety artist. He had also served five substantial prison sentences, twice for forgery and three times for theft.

He alone was imprisoned for the Croydon Airport robbery. Doubtless he was well rewarded on release by those whose names he had not mentioned.

It had been a simple walk-in for the thieves. They had known exactly what the security arrangements were; they had a key. Was any one of the three key holders responsible for this?

And another question. Why did Little Harry hire a taxi to take the gang to Purley Way. Why at such short notice? And why select such a broken reed as George Manson who needed to be very seriously threatened after making such a revealing statement to the police?

And who were the thieves? O'Brien? His name never came up in later suggestions. Probably he was not involved. The best bet, according to underworld whispers, was Little Harry Sabini (see 'A Day at the Races') and the boxer Bert Marsh (real name Pasquale Poppa). They were suspected of the robbery but were never charged. One wonders why. And, of course, the stylish ladies' man, Silvio 'Shonk' Mazzarda, was a leading member of the Sabini gang. He liked the high life, the fast cars – he was the gang's getaway driver – but he also participated in the Battle of the Nile, a 1920s' gunfight that took place when the Titanic Mob from Hoxton met the Sabinis in Nile Street. Apparently even Silvio's razor-slashed cheek did not detract from his attractivness.

The Underworld scored heavily in this case and certainly for the loss of only one man made an enormous haul. One Sabini bookie, a man in the know, began betting under the name of Nick Gold. Just another joke of course.

THE CUTT MILL MURDER

———————— ❀ ————————

It was Robin Huber who found the body. Poor young lad, only 14 years old. Small wonder that he dashed straight home. He'd gone along to Heath Cottage at eight o'clock that Saturday morning as he usually did to look after the geese and ducks and pigs and he'd just walked into the scullery and there she was, lying there. He hadn't any experience of dead bodies but he knew that Mrs Keen was beyond all help.

Young Huber, breathless, told his mother what he had found, that he had seen old Annie Keen on the scullery floor, that he was sure she was dead, and they sent for the police.

And Albert Keen hadn't turned up for work that day, Saturday, 8 October 1932. He was employed as foreman up at Rodsall Manor, the home of Sir Lawrence and Lady Guillemard, on the Puttenham to Shackleford road. He was such a steady worker, well known in the area as a reliable man. But where was he? It was so unlike him not to come to work. They sent the chauffeur down to see where he was and he came back to the Manor with such a terrible tale about poor Annie. And still Albert was nowhere to be found. Was he responsible for what had happened to his wife?

Strange, but the most apparently loving husbands do dispose of their wives. Whoever would have thought that Albert Keen was capable of such a wicked deed? They had been such a devoted pair. But it is a sad fact that the majority of murders are committed by family members. It just showed that even in the case of the closest of couples you never could tell.

Then, some time later in the morning, Albert's body was found in Cutt Mill Pond, only 400 yards or so from his home. He appeared to be standing upright, his mouth just under the water.

There were wounds to the back of his head, which the police believed had been sustained when, jumping into the pond, he had struck tree stumps under the surface of the water. He had murdered his wife and remorseful had committed suicide. At least, that was the immediate and most obvious conclusion.

When, during the course of the morning, Detective Sergeant Curry and PC Tom Roberts arrived at Heath Cottage it was to investigate a murder and a suicide. They found Annie Keen lying where Robin Huber had left her. It was not surprising that the boy had run home for the scene was horrific. There were eight cuts to the woman's throat, one of them so deep and violent that it had gone through to the backbone. And there had been three savage blows to the head from where blood seeped onto the floor. Beside the body lay a sharpening stone and an ordinary kitchen knife, its blade bloodied. There was no doubt that the knife was the murder weapon but perhaps the stone had first been used to cosh her, to beat her to the ground.

Bloodstains on the door suggested that Annie had been attacked in the kitchen and her body then dragged into the scullery. Or perhaps she had staggered there in an attempt to escape from her assailant.

The detectives noted that the table was laid and on it were a cocoa tin and a bottle of vinegar. But a pan of fish was cold. It had been cooked hours earlier and never served. It was obvious from this that the murder had occurred some time on the previous day.

In the inspection of the house the detectives found a chest of drawers in the living room containing two empty purses. Upstairs in one of the bedrooms they discovered that the locks on two wooden chests had been forced. Both were empty. This began to look more like a burglary. Would a man who had murdered his wife burgle his own cottage?

Tom Roberts, then only a constable, was to be the founder of Surrey CID. And at the lonely Cutt Mill cottage he had an early opportunity to demonstrate his forensic skills. In those days there was no training for detectives. They picked up the elements of their work from more experienced officers and if it chanced that their colleagues were not terribly efficient, then the process of learning was all the more difficult. But Roberts was by nature

methodical, thorough, and deeply interested in his work. Evidence
of this lies in the photographs he took at various crime scenes in
the course of what was to become a distinguished career. And at
Heath Cottage he photographed everything. Using his own old-
fashioned flash camera he took shots of the exterior of the house,
the rooms, the wooden chests, the knife, the sharpening stone, the
body lying in the scullery. And then in the bathroom back at his
lodgings, Roberts developed the film. On that October Saturday,
only hours after the murder of Annie Keen, forensic photography
in the Surrey Constabulary was born in a damp little cottage that
had neither electricity nor mains water. Heath Cottage was a
picturesque enough place, isolated, with its pig-pen just inside the
gate and the chicken run opposite and a tall thick hedge bordering
the large garden. But it seems an odd spot for such a significant
change in detective work.

For the investigating officers there was little to go on
immediately. There were no identifiable fingerprints save those of
the Keens. And despite the pool of blood at Annie's head and the
stains on the kitchen door there was less blood than might have
been expected. There was a theory at the time that whoever had
murdered Annie was familiar with the methods employed by
animal slaughterers and this was supported by the police doctor.

While Curry and Roberts were busy at Heath Cottage, others
were at Cutt Mill Pond. A brick tied to a piece of cord was found
near the track by the pond. Was this some kind of weapon? And
a cudgel was spotted floating in the water. Was this another
weapon? And there were other hints that Albert Keen had been a
victim. His macintosh had been found on the banks of the pond.
The sleeves were partly inside out as if he had struggled to take off
the garment in order to defend himself better.

The police continued to drag the pond with a cast-iron grapnel.
They brought up a basket containing a bottle of milk. Significant?
Certainly it was. Albert always brought home milk from the dairy,
every day, without fail. When he finished work at Rodsall Manor
he used to take the 15 minutes walk home by the rough cart track
along the side of the millpond. Then he would cut through the
woods and over the Shackleford road to Heath Cottage. And he
always brought his basket of milk from the dairy. But there was

Heath Cottage, Cutt Mill, where the body of Annie Keen was found in the scullery.

no milk in the house on the Saturday morning. Because after leaving work on the Friday he had not reached home. Annie had been waiting for him, the meal nearly prepared. He had left work at the usual time and got no further than Cutt Mill Pond. As they searched the pond and the bushes nearby the police found unmistakable signs that someone had been hiding in the bushes, waiting there. Waiting for Albert.

The bodies were taken to Godalming mortuary for the post mortem. Dr James Milligan, the police surgeon, was certain that Albert had not committed suicide for there were three wounds to the back of his head. The doctor concluded that he had been the victim of a surprise attack and that he had tumbled into the water, perhaps stunned by the blows. He gave the cause of death as drowning.

This then was a double murder and for Surrey Police it was a major case. They had experienced nothing like it since the investigation into the disappearance of Agatha Christie five years earlier.

But why would anyone wish to murder these people? No one had a bad word for them. They were described as 'affectionate and cheerful' and 'a nice old couple' – Albert was 61, Annie 54 – with no enemies. They had been seen earlier on the Friday and appeared to have no troubles of any kind. They were so well known. They belonged here. Albert had been born at Heath Cottage, and the house had been occupied by members of his family for more than a hundred years. He had always been employed locally. Until the early part of the year he had worked at Cutt Mill House for Mr Alan Nobes, subsequently moving just a short distance away to Rodsall Manor.

What could have been the motive for this horrific killing? Money? It was said that Albert did not use banks, that he hadn't deposited money in a bank for the last thirty years. Nothing surprising in that. There were many working men who felt the same. And if you lived in an out-of-the-way place like Cutt Mill you wouldn't be inclined to go all the way to town to bank your earnings. So where did people keep their money? In the house? But where? Under the bed? Locked up in a chest? Under the floorboards? They had to put it somewhere. And some people were of the view that the Keens had a considerable amount of money hidden in the house. After all, they had no children, had they? And they bought and sold livestock, didn't they? And he'd never been out of work. Stood to reason, there must be a tidy sum.

So then if it was a double murder, who had been murdered first? Was it Annie in the cottage or Albert as he walked by the water's edge? Roberts and his colleagues were soon of the opinion that it was Annie who had been the first victim. Their surmise was that the murderer had started by going to the cottage. But for what reason? He had used a kitchen knife from the house to kill her. Presumably he had not gone there with the intention of murdering her otherwise he would have gone armed. Had she surprised him breaking open the chests and had he then turned on her? Or perhaps he had gone to the cottage and she had asked him in? Did Annie already know her killer? It was a quiet enough place, not easily discovered by strangers. And, come to think of it, would a stranger know that the Keens were believed to have a significant sum of money in the house?

And then, the police thought, the killer had gone to the pond and had hidden himself in the bushes until Albert came by on his way from work. Presumably he did not wish the alarm to be raised straightaway. But how did he know the time when Albert would be coming home? How did he know the way he would come? It all pointed to someone with local knowledge, someone who knew the Keens. And it also pointed to an unplanned murder. Perhaps someone had gone there with the intention of burgling the house and then matters had got out of hand.

The police questioned Norman Vessey, the Hampton Estate gamekeeper, who at the time of the murder had seen two men in the wood. They had had a cocker spaniel with them. Vessey had kept an eye on them in case they were poachers. They had driven off in a small two-seater car. All subsequent attempts by the police to identify these men failed. Vessey also mentioned a man in his thirties whom he had met in the woods at about 5.30 pm. He did not know him but then the gamekeeper had only recently moved into the district. He described the man as wearing a blue suit and a light grey felt trilby. He had asked Vessey the whereabouts of the nearest stop for the Guildford bus.

On 20 October Vessey was called to an identity parade and pointed out to the police the man he had spoken to in the wood. It was Godfrey Nobes, who gave his current address as the Princess Royal public house up on the Hog's Back at Runfold. For some days he had been in custody on a charge of fraudulently obtaining from another local man a banker's cheque valued at £4 10 shillings.

On Friday 21 October Nobes was charged with the murder of Annie and Albert Keen. Until recently the Nobes family had lived at Cutt Mill House where Albert had worked as cowman until Alan Nobes died and his wife sold up the property.

And it must have seemed a watertight case. For Godfrey Nobes, 31 years old, son of a one-time prosperous dairy farmer, was universally disliked in the neighbourhood and was known as a waster, a man whose family had despaired of him. Only twelve months or so earlier his mother had given him £400, then a significant sum, but he had spent it and had run into debt. Nobes was now engaged to 18 year old Gladys Hook whose mother was the licensee of the Princess Royal where he was lodging, about five miles away. Mrs Hook charged him 12 shillings and sixpence a week for his board and lodgings but on 7 October he owed her £2 15 6d for back rent.

And Nobes had been attempting to borrow money for several days prior to the murder. Not that there was anything new about that. One man who had worked at Cutt Mill House farm when Godfrey Nobes was the overseer there told how Nobes had tried to borrow £20 from him. More recently, the licensee of the Bricklayers Arms in Farnham said that on the very day of the murder, Nobes had asked to borrow £1 from him but he had refused. The manager of the fishmonger's shop at Farnborough also spoke about being asked for money. He had been foolish enough to lend Nobes £1 but had not seen him since. Another man told the police that he knew that Godfrey Nobes had been pestering the Keens to lend him money.

Was that why he had been seen at the Keens' cottage earlier in the week? Had he been trying to borrow money then? Not at all, Nobes told the police. He had been there to buy some geese. A point worth pursuing? Certainly. Because men short of cash do not try to buy geese. But this aspect of the investigation seems not to have been followed up by the police. But they did wonder how this man, so desperate for cash, was able to pay £2 towards his overdue rent on the day after the murder.

And then there was the matter of Nobes' bloodstained clothing. When he was arrested his jacket, trousers, waistcoat and trilby were sent for forensic examination. Blood was found in 96 separate places on the jacket, the waistcoat, and the trousers. There were eight other small splashes of blood on the trilby. And what about the throat wounds that Dr Milligan likened to the way in which animals are slaughtered? Until recently Nobes had lived and worked all his life on a farm.

And of course he did not deny that he had been in the wood near Heath Cottage at about the time of the murder. He had taken a bus from Sandy Cross to Shoelands corner, arriving there at 3.45 pm. He admitted to not having any bus fare and said that he had told the driver he would pay his fare on the return journey. He had walked towards Cutt Mill by way of Hillbury. He remembered speaking to Vessey at about 5.30 after which he had walked on to Shackleford. He was just filling in time, Nobes explained to the police. His fiancée and her mother believed him to be working in a pork butcher's shop in Farnborough but he had taken the day off. He claimed to have gone to his old home, Cutt Mill House, which was being converted into a country residence and he wanted to see it in daylight. In fact he had spent much of the day aimlessly wandering, cadging where he could, and drinking at Farnham and Ash.

Nobes could not have gone to Heath Cottage before five o'clock because there were builders working there. If he had committed the murders, then he had killed Annie after the builders left, had subsequently met Vessey, and had murdered Albert at about 5.45 pm. The police believed that Nobes had enough time to kill both victims.

Godfrey Nobes began his three-day trial before Mr Justice Hawke at the Surrey Assizes in Kingston on 10 December 1932.

Albert and Annie Keen.

The prosecution case was that Nobes knew the habits of Mr and Mrs Keen, that he had gone there to steal their money and that he had murdered Annie and then, to give himself enough time to escape, he had felt obliged to murder her husband.

The blood evidence was crucial to the prosecution case. Yet it was insufficiently convincing. The day after the murder, Godfrey Nobes' suit was washed by his fiancée. Not that she was trying to conceal a crime. It was simply that the suit was in need of cleaning because of his nosebleeds and because it was spattered with mud. Nobes' defence produced evidence that he was subject to regular nosebleeds. Perhaps unconsciously he had passed his hand across his nose and transferred the blood to his hat and clothes. 'I have lost as much as a teacupful at a time and have bled as much as two or three times a week,' he told the police. Or there was another possibility. Perhaps the blood came from a rabbit. 'Where the rabbits hang at the Princess Royal is where I hang my hat and Mrs Hook has washed clothes belonging to me there that have been soaked with blood.'

But Godfrey Nobes said none of these things in court. When the case for the prosecution ended all eyes turned towards the accused man. Then came an incident that heightened the tension and for which no one was prepared. Mr W.R. Manley, defence counsel, rose from his seat and instead of commencing his address or calling the accused he said, 'My lord, the prisoner has a statement to make to the jury. I have no other evidence to call.'

'Mr Manley,' the judge replied, 'you know as well as I do what that decision involves.'

Indeed, for it is never safe for an accused not to face the questions of the prosecution.

But Godfrey Nobes then advanced to the front of the dock and, speaking calmly, he said, 'Ladies and gentlemen, I am not guilty of either of these murders. When I was arrested by the police I told them everything I knew. Everything I said was true.'

And he sat down.

But Mr Manley for the defence dissected the evidence meticulously, pointing out the weak links in the chain of circumstances by which the prosecution sought to connect Nobes with the crime. He said that the jury would see that it was a 'rotten, weak and knock-kneed case'. Manley touched on the possibility that Albert Keen might have killed his wife and then have thrown himself into the pond. 'Is it impossible to suppose that after Keen's arrival home some disagreement occurred between him and his wife? Maybe his wife struck him on the head and then, in a fit of insane frenzy, he fell upon her and murdered her. Mechanically, he takes the road along which he travels every day. He reaches the corner, trips over something, and falls onto those snags. It is an unlikely explanation but is it incredible? Nobody knows. All sorts of things support the suggestion that it is not incredible.'

And add to that the fact that Albert's mentally unstable sister had on more than one occasion tried to commit suicide by throwing herself from the wall into the pond.

Mr Manley also dwelt particularly upon the weakness of the evidence of the bloodstains. It was impossible, he said, to tell if the bloodstains were one week or ten years old. As for the police failure to produce the two motorists seen by Vessey in the woods, Manley said it was plain as a pikestaff that the motorists had something to hide. Would they not have come forward if they had nothing to conceal, he asked.

Summing up, Mr Justice Hawke warned the jury against being prejudiced by Nobes' decision not to go into the witness box. The jury must be satisfied, he insisted, beyond all reasonable doubt that Nobes was the murderer. If they were not, then he was entitled to an acquittal. With regard to the bloodstains, the judge said, 'I do not know whether I have ever fully understood the blood side of this case,' adding that, 'I should like to take you into my confidence on that.'

The jury was out a mere 45 minutes. They returned with a unanimous not guilty verdict.

Immediately after hearing the judgement, Nobes left the area, deserting his fiancée in the process. Some say that he set himself up in Kent as a fruit farmer under an assumed name. Others have suggested that he went to Australia. But nothing definite has emerged of his subsequent history from the moment he stepped out of the courtroom.

The police never reopened the case. All was forgotten. Forgotten, that is, until 2002, when a Fulcrum TV programme,

Unsolved Murders, on the Discovery Channel, resurrected the case. The barrister Anthony Scrivener re-examined the murder with the help of forensic experts, using scientific techniques that were not available to Tom Roberts and his colleagues seventy years earlier. There were two major factors for the modern investigators to consider. The first was the timing of the murder. Did Nobes have enough time to kill both people? This had been considered by Roberts and his colleagues and they had concluded that he had had time. Anthony Scrivener's team arrived at the same conclusion.

But what about the blood evidence? Today DNA would have resolved the matter. In 1932 the jury, though its members might have been dubious about Nobes' innocence, was unconvinced by the blood evidence. Although there were 96 separate specks of blood on his clothing, the prosecution could not prove that all were human. And in any case, Nobes suffered from nosebleeds so that what stains there were might well have been his. Or perhaps they had come from the pork butcher's shop in which he was intermittently working.

And what about the eight miniscule spots on his trilby hat? Initially Nobes had said that they possibly came from rabbits hanging up in the Princess Royal. When they were proved to be human, Nobes asserted that they must be his own. But Scrivener's forensic experts were confident that the infinitesimal specks of blood resulted from the savage blows delivered by the sharpening stone. These were splashes thrown upwards from Annie Keen as she lay on the floor helpless while Nobes stabbed and stabbed and stabbed her. Today's experts have no doubt about the guilt of Godfrey Nobes.

It seems that at last, though now too late, a great Surrey murder mystery has been resolved.

OPERATION YAMOTO

———————— ❀ ————————

Four minutes at the Texaco Service Station at Woodhatch, that's all it took. Just four minutes on the morning of Tuesday, 27 November 1990, where shoppers were making their way along the Parade and mothers with their youngest children were on their way to the Clinic while elderly energetics were taking their early morning walk.

At 9.55 am a Securicor van pulled up in the garage forecourt and two of the guards, Ray Tuck and June Wheeler, climbed out. They often made a stop here for coffee at the café behind the garage and this morning was no different. They had just made their usual call at the post office round the corner and it was now time for a break. Unscheduled, by the way, as far as their managers were concerned. But the crew had their own routines.

Inside the van, the third member, Brian Delamere, waited for the other two to bring him his polystyrene mug of coffee. After that they'd be on their way to their other calls. They still had £750,000 in the van.

At 9.57 am, just when Tuck and Wheeler were about to get back into the van, a red, open-backed Nissan truck, its headlights full on, pulled into the forecourt. And without warning a man wearing a grotesque party mask with the face of an old man jumped out and pointed a pistol at the two guards. He shouted at them to get back into their van straightaway, warning them that if they resisted they would be shot.

Almost simultaneously three others, all armed, had emerged from the Nissan. They were frightening to look at. One wore an Afro wig with large black spectacle frames, another also wore party spectacles, his face blacked with boot polish, while the face of the third was concealed under a caricature Ronald Reagan mask.

'Afro Wig' and 'Reagan' gave armed cover, warning off any member of the public courageous enough or perhaps foolish enough to intervene. The other two bundled the three guards into the back of the security van, the 'Old Man' climbing in with them, keeping his gun trained on them. At this point 'Afro Wig' jumped into the driving seat of the Securicor van, preparing to drive off while 'Boot Polish' and 'Reagan' jumped into the Nissan, intending to follow. Obviously they meant to drive to some secluded spot where they had a getaway car waiting.

This was a swiftly executed, obviously well-planned robbery. And by 9.59 am, after a mere four minutes, it was all over. But by then matters had changed. There had been a dramatic intervention. Guns had been fired. One man lay wounded on the forecourt. A second man had been killed.

For the most part, by the late 1980s the so-called Golden Age of Armed Robbery was over. Major criminal activity had turned towards massive tax and VAT frauds, often involving crooked dealings in gold and major investments in drugs. But not everyone cared for these types of crimes. They didn't set the blood running. There was no adrenalin rush for those involved. And anyway, gold and drugs required heavy initial expenditure. For some it was no more thrilling than accountancy, no more exciting than driving a delivery van. No, for some, armed robbery was the best way, the most thrilling way, of making a living. There was a buzz about it. And if guns went off and someone was unfortunate enough to be killed, well, there was no hanging any more. And if the heist went wrong and they were caught they'd receive heavy sentences, armed or not. So why not carry a gun, even if it was just to frighten people off? And if they weren't frightened off, well ... 'Yesterday's men', they were sometimes called. But some 'yesterday's men' in the course of a Securicor van raid at Dartford in 1976 had killed David Cross, a security guard, and had gone off with £103,000, firing at passers-by who had attempted to pursue them; in another armed raid in 1987 two men had been killed; and over the years there had been several other deaths and many serious injuries.

And so to Woodhatch where 'yesterday's men' of 1990 had turned up for the job armed for serious business. Between them

THE TIMES TUESDAY DECEMBER 10 1991

'Ruthless' raiders jailed for armed Securicor robbery

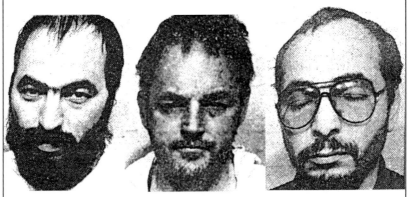

Dennis Arif: disguised as an old man

Downer: related to the Arif clan by marriage

Mehmet Arif: drove stolen pickup truck

they carried a 12 gauge pump-action sawn-off shotgun, a .38 revolver, a .45 self-loading pistol and a 9 mm self-loading pistol. All had live ammunition.

But the waiting police, Scotland Yard and Flying Squad men, supported by specialist marksmen, were ready too.

For the past year police had been investigating a series of armed robberies in Surrey and Kent and they had had a shrewd idea of who the robbers were. And just as the gang kept discreet watch on vans carrying bullion, they in turn were watched by police. Just as the robbers knew the official routines of the Securicor vans and the individual habits of their teams, so did the watching police officers know their quarry, keeping them under close observation, using telephone bugs, homing devices and the usual underworld informants. By the late summer of 1990 the police were sure that Woodhatch was a likely spot for an attack on a Securicor vehicle although they were aware that the gang had scouted out two other possible vans and locations. Any one of three vans could be the target. Two weeks earlier police officers had been prepared for the robbery and had waited at Woodhatch for the gang but nothing had occurred. But on the evening of 26 November there was a strong indication that the Woodhatch drop would be targeted on the following day, because that evening a stolen car was driven by a gang member to a secluded spot near Woodhatch. It was obviously a getaway vehicle.

On the morning of 27 November, only a minute or so after the robbers jumped out of their Nissan truck, Operation Yamoto, named after the unexpected Japanese attack on Pearl Harbour, swung into action.

Detective Chief Inspector Mike Brooker, the officer in charge of Yamoto, was positioned in a first-floor flat that overlooked the service station and he was in contact by radio with his force of hidden policemen. When he saw the robbers pile out of the Nissan he gave orders to his men to apprehend them.

At 9.58 am, the gang was preparing to drive off, satisfied that their operation had been carried out with the usual maximum efficiency. And then came the screeching tyres of four squad cars and other surveillance vehicles. Out of these tumbled 30 policemen, 14 of them armed with semi-automatic pistols, revolvers or rifles.

When Detective Sergeant Terry Hobbs drove his unmarked black saloon up to the bumper of the Nissan, 'Reagan' and 'Boot Polish,' in the front seats, were unable to drive off the forecourt. Police marksman PC William Hughes opened the Nissan passenger door. There was a shout of 'Freeze. Armed police.' And then 'Reagan' swivelled in his seat, levelling his semi-automatic in the direction of the shout. Hughes fired, hitting the man in the stomach. At the trial he said, 'I felt a muzzle blast across the left side of my face and realised that the man in the passenger seat was shooting at me and I could tell my life was in danger. I fired two shots at him and then I heard two shots on my left and saw the passenger window disintegrate.' One of his colleagues, aware of the robbers' intention, fired at 'Reagan' through the passenger side window. The bullet hit him in the mouth and pierced his skull and he died instantly. 'Boot Polish' in the driving seat was hit in the shoulder by a second rifle round but he, fortunately, was wearing body armour. It all occurred in a matter of seconds.

The two shot robbers fell out of their car onto the garage forecourt where they lay in a pool of blood. Their two companions, 'Old Man' and 'Afro Wig,' inside the Securicor van, put up no resistance. How could they? They could not drive away because a police vehicle had rammed the front of their van and they were now surrounded by the team of police marksmen from Scotland Yard's PT 17 firearms unit. Both robbers threw down their guns and were at once handcuffed and driven to Reigate police station.

All this sudden, short, hectic activity was against a soundtrack of shouts, barked orders and the anxious calls of passers-by who, shocked by the sudden outbreak of violence, scrambled to safety inside the shops.

But rather than congratulate themselves on the thwarting of a major criminal enterprise, within minutes senior Surrey officers gathered in the Chief Superintendent's wood-panelled room to discuss the ramifications of a robber's death in their area. Shortly afterwards senior members of the Flying Squad's operation arrived, followed by a representative of the Police Complaints Authority. Superintendent Pat Crossan, a very experienced Surrey officer, was appointed by the PCA to head an enquiry into the shooting.

The following year the three robbers were tried at the Old Bailey. This was a high profile trial of men described as 'first division London villains'. Two of them, brothers, belonged to a well-known criminal family, the Arifs, Turkish Cypriots who lived in Rotherhithe and were the most heavily investigated criminal gang since the Krays. At Woodhatch they had suffered a severe setback. One of the gang members, 53 year old Kenneth Baker, a well-known criminal, who had worn the 'Reagan' mask, was dead and Mehmet Arif ('Boot Polish') was wounded and two more, Dennis Arif ('Old Man') and Anthony Downer ('Afro Wig'), were in custody.

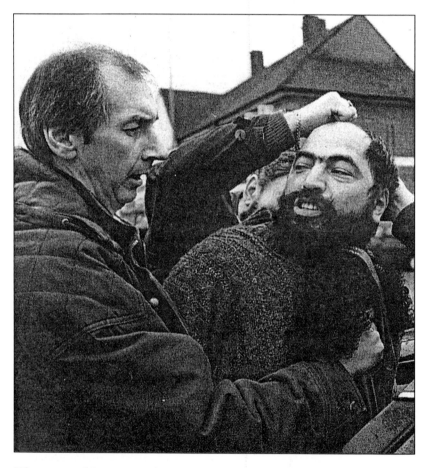

The arrest of Dennis Arif.

The Arifs first appeared as major criminals in the 1970s and now, nearly twenty years later, as a consequence of many successful armed robberies, they were owners of a variety of clubs, pubs and restaurants in south east London. 'It doesn't matter whose name is over the door of the pub in some areas,' it was said, 'it's the Arifs who own it.' Over the years they had gained ascendancy over other local gangs by their sheer ruthlessness. They had overcome all resistance by being harder, quicker thinking and better organised. And crime certainly paid. In turn, from time to time, family members paid their dues to society. Head of the family and one-time owner of Fisher Athletic Football Club, Dogan Arif, one of seven brothers, was gaoled in 1985 for his part in a £8.8 million cannabis smuggling racket. Ozer, another brother, who had served a prison sentence for robbery, was charged and acquitted of the 1976 murder of security guard David Cross at Dartford. Bekir Arif served five years after being found guilty of disposing of the guns used in this robbery. Now Dennis Arif, 35, allegedly a jeweller, sentenced to 11 years in 1981 for conspiracy to rob, and his brother Mehmet, a Dulwich restaurateur, who had been wounded at Woodhatch, were to face the court along with their brother-in-law, Anthony Downer, a Catford builder.

The Arifs' notorious reputation led Mr Michael Stuart-Moore for the prosecution to ask for jury protection. The Arifs, he said, were 'by no means unknown to the police' and had considerable power and influence in terms of money and muscle. 'There is every likelihood', Mr Stuart-Moore said, 'that if protection is not granted the defendants' family, or associates, will attempt to interfere one way or another with the jury. They have done it before and they are quite capable of doing it again.' This was a reference to a previous trial in 1981, when Dennis and his brother Bekir were before the court for armed robbery, and members of the family and their associates had hung about outside the court, intimidating jurors. One female juror was approached by an unknown woman who offered her money to engineer a 'not guilty' verdict. After she reported this she was given police protection as were four other equally frightened jury members.

This time during the two-week trial there were heavy security measures with armed officers guarding the court and escorting the gang members to and from prison each day. A police squad, 72 members strong, gave 24-hour protection to the jury. As one detective confided to the *Independent*: 'The Arifs are undoubtedly feared. People are not daft enough to cross them.'

At their trial Mehmet and Downer both pleaded guilty. Dennis Arif, however, who asked unsuccessfully if he might be tried under another name for fear of jury prejudice, offered a most remarkable story in his defence. Despite being caught in the act, he pleaded not guilty to conspiracy to rob. He had been, he said, forced into taking part in the robbery. According to him, he owed Baker £60,000 in gambling debts and Baker had threatened to shoot him, he said, if he did not pay up. Admittedly, Dennis might well have owed Baker a considerable sum of money – it was said that over the previous 20 years gambling had cost him £100,000 and more recently he had lost £15,000 at a London casino – but the truth seemed to be that the men were close friends. Only months before the Woodhatch robbery both had attended the wedding of a family member at the Savoy that had cost £32,000. The revelation of such conspicuous expenditure was unlikely to have roused the jury's sympathies, especially when it emerged that Dennis lived in an East London council house.

Before sentencing the men, Mehmet Arif and Downer to 18 years and Dennis Arif to 22 years, the judge, Mrs Heather Steel, observed, 'You are each dangerous, ruthless, greedy and clever men from whom society must be protected for a very long time. You were going as four armed men to take care of three unarmed security guards in charge of a large sum of money. I have no doubt when you went out that morning you were each prepared to shoot and be shot at. The way you went armed and prepared, you anticipated armed police may be involved and you were prepared for an armed shoot-out.'

At the end of the trial one of the detectives involved in the case said, 'We reckoned they made millions. We believe they have been active armed robbers for about 20 years. Every job was always meticulously planned and ruthlessly executed.'

There were suggestions at the time – though whether or not there was any foundation for these is unclear – that the

Woodhatch robbery was masterminded by Dogan Arif from his prison. With the money from this raid some considered that he might have intended to finance an escape plan.

After the trial an inquest on Kenneth Baker produced a verdict of 'lawful killing'. The jury were told that two police marksmen opened fire on Baker after he pointed his gun at one of the constables.

Superintendent Pat Crossan's independent investigation into the death of Kenneth Baker supported the police action. 'There was every possibility that the gang would try to shoot themselves out of trouble,' the Superintendent said. Nevertheless, the shooting of Kenneth Baker revived the debate about whether British police should be regularly armed. In recent years at least half a dozen criminals have been killed by armed police in similar operations. A distinct majority of police is against general arming but there is a strong case for specialist marksmen. Newspapers and television pictures regularly feature heavily armed, flak-jacketed officers protecting courts, watching over state occasions or patrolling airport concourses. There is an evident need for such precautions. In the main, professional criminals do not go armed but where they do they are perhaps best combated by men equipped equally powerfully. But the matter at this stage is still very far from resolution.

Finally and as a footnote, it is said that Dogan Arif was rather upset in the year 2000 when he was relegated to seventh place in the *Sunday Times* 'Criminal Rich List'. He attributed his poor showing to his current limiting circumstances.

EXOTIC FRUITS

———————— ❁ ————————

They read like a poem, these words: guavas and passion fruit, peaches and avocados, mangoes, chayote and hot, hot peppers. And they look like a painting, all these exotic fruits, their reds, yellows, deep plums, greens and delicate pinks, shipped all the way here to Britain from Lima. We have an increasing passion for the exotic, the foreign, and the Black brothers with their fruit importing business, Marishal, at Smithbrook Kilns on the Cranleigh to Guildford road, were among those responding to our needs. Guillermo Black back in Lima sent regular shipments to his brothers, Rene and Rudi, and how well the business seemed to be doing to judge by the affluence the two young South Americans displayed. They had all the Latin dash and flair that was perhaps expected of them. They were themselves appropriately exotic characters.

Rene and Rudi Black had arrived in Britain in 1982 and were soon established in Surrey. Rene was rated fifth among Peruvian show jumpers. That was sufficient entrée to the social circles in which he liked to move. He had come here to improve his competitive skills but in this country he was not an especially successful competitor, rated merely at 58. However, he opened a show jumping centre at Pollingfold, his luxury home at Ellen's Green, which had extensive stables and on which he laid out at least £500,000. This confirmed his place in Surrey society.

And the rather dashing Rudi, who lived in Guildford and had interests in sports car racing on which he spent up to £120,000 a year, was equally in demand. The brothers, so obviously from a moneyed South American family, fitted easily into the affluent society around them. They had both purchased very expensive penthouses in Miami. At Ellen's Green, Rene, bringing his home up to date, spent £90,000 on his new kitchen. In cash.

Theirs was a playboy lifestyle lived in a world of fast cars (their driveways sported a Mazda RX7, a Porsche 911 Carrera, some or other Mercedes), frequent foreign travel (always first class), expensive restaurants and casinos. And always there were women, stable girls from Cranleigh and round about, croupiers from London clubs and others from all reaches of society, both in this country and the rest of the world, and all enjoying the company of the high-spending Peruvians. Money, it seemed, was no object to either man. What a dazzling pair they were.

It was during these years that Rene was divorced from his first wife and in 1988 married a local girl, 19 year old Michelle, whose elder sister, Dawn, was to marry Rudi though theirs was a short-lived association. Rudi's somewhat rackety lifestyle constantly led him into the arms of other women.

Rene now moved house a short way from Pollingfold to Fairfield, an equally expensive property. He had given up his stables and begun investing in racing cars.

And the exotic fruit business continued to pay off, funding the high-roller lifestyle of the two young men. But not for ever. Their empire was to crash.

It is unclear if Surrey Police had any inkling about the Black brothers' activities before 13 August 1988. Possibly they had known that two men, James Laming, a Peckham car dealer, and Patrick Fraser, were dealing in drugs. But did they already know who was supplying them? Perhaps not. In any event, on the day when Fraser and Laming were arrested outside a London pub, the good times were about to end for the brothers Black.

Fraser had been found in possession of a half kilo of cocaine worth £100,000 as well as £1,000 in cash. 'I suppose it had to happen sooner or later. This is what happens when you get greedy,' he is alleged to have said to the police. A further £21,000 was found at his home. On the same occasion Laming is said to have remarked to the men who arrested him, 'You have caught us bang to rights.' He too had a half kilo of cocaine.

And perhaps it was then that for the first time Rene and Rudi Black came under surveillance by the Surrey Police although the National Drugs Intelligence Unit was already aware of their activities. Banks are obliged to alert police to the suspicious

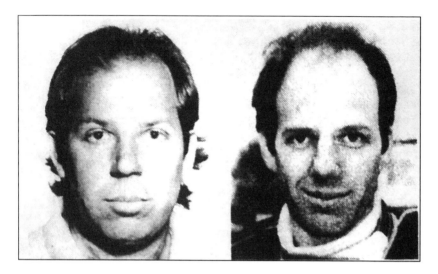

Rene and Rudi Black.

movements of money that they believe could be drug-related. Bank officials had noted that the brothers regularly changed notes of relatively small denominations into £50 notes. Sometimes as much as £30,000 was changed in this way. Why should they want to do this? Was it to make it easier to carry money out of the country? Were they involved in some kind of money laundering? And such huge sums too. Could fruit imports really produce such great profits? The banks related their concerns to the Drugs Squad. Even before the arrest of Laming and Fraser, the NDIU, if not the Surrey Police, were gathering intelligence on the Marishal Fruit Company and its owners.

Operation Peninsula was the crucial two-month surveillance exercise by detectives engaged in the drugs war, which culminated in their closing down the first laboratory refining raw cocaine known to have been established in Europe. During September and October 1988, the Black brothers were under close observation. Undercover officers hid in trees and bushes for days on end to watch every move at Fairfield. The brothers were constantly shadowed. Rene was followed to the Sure Store container park at an industrial estate near Heathrow. Here, investigators found that containers Nos 65 and 28 were rented out in the name of DeNegri; the firm could apparently be contacted on the Marishal phone number.

In November 1988, when the police were satisfied that the time was right, the containers were smashed open. Various items of drug-processing equipment were found: glassware, five fermenting bins and 30 kilograms of cocaine valued at £5 million in plastic bags. The raw cocaine had been brought into the country concealed in the hollowed-out wooden pallets that had carried mangoes and avocados and all the other fruits from the Lima-based company run by Guillermo Black. The discovery of suitcases containing cash totalling £400,000 gave the police their first real idea of the size of their haul.

Rene Black was arrested but his brother Rudi was in Miami with one of the Surrey stable girls and so he escaped capture. On money-laundering transatlantic flights about £218,000 had already been taken into the United States en route for banks in Panama. Presumably this was the principal reason why, at the moment of his brother's arrest, Rudi was in Miami.

At the factory at Fairfield, Rene's new home at Ellen's Green, it was discovered that he had produced and planned to flood Britain with 180 kilograms of cocaine with a market value of £15.5 million.

But treachery and drug trafficking go hand in hand. Whatever rung they occupy on the ladder those employed in the trade are rarely able to rely on those above or below them. From the most humble street dealer upwards, from the drugs baron downwards, at the end, when the going gets tough, they frequently sell each other out. And so Rene Black, millionaire, realising his position, admitting to having masterminded and financed Europe's first known cocaine factory and, acknowledging that he would receive a very long prison sentence, informed on his distributors whom he named as Laming, Fraser and Martin Cox, a Chessington man. He hoped that his cooperation would be given some consideration when it came to sentencing.

And so it came about that in Southwark Crown Court in August 1989, 34 year old Rene Pedro Black pleaded guilty to conspiring to import cocaine into Britain between March 1986 and November 1988; conspiring to produce cocaine hydrochloride between the same dates; conspiring to supply cocaine between January 1987 and 19 August 1988 and possessing 30 kilos of cocaine worth £5 million in November 1988 with intent to supply.

For the defence Mr Ivan Lawrence explained that his client had made frank admissions which would be helpful to the prosecution. In due course, Mr Lawrence said, Black would make further statements.

For the prosecution Mr Andrew Mitchell told the court that the object of the matter being brought before the court was to facilitate the defendant making pleas of guilty and to allow him to start making the statements to be used against the three other defendants – Fraser, Laming and Cox – accused of being involved in importing and dealing in Peruvian cocaine. Their trial was to start on 16 October.

As a supergrass, Rene Black was now in danger. There was said to be a £1 million contract out on his life. The court was told that after he agreed to turn Queen's evidence, he had said to the police, 'I know I am in Hell. I know I am lost.' Throughout the trial in October 1989, every day before the court opened, the room was searched by sniffer dogs. Armed police officers wearing flak jackets were posted inside and outside the court. For his protection Black was often flown to court by helicopter and it was already agreed that he would spend his inevitable prison sentence in isolation.

Black did not appear in the witness box although his statements were frequently referred to. He had admitted to all of the charges brought against him but, as if in mitigation, he had told the police that the drug was intended for sale to wealthy members of society. 'This stupid drug is for people who have lots of money to pay for it. It is not for children in the streets or people like that.' But such an exclusive market is unlikely, for Black had no control over his distributors or their clients.

The court was informed of how Black had made huge profits from smuggling raw cocaine from Peru. Normally cocaine is shipped already 'cut down' which reduces its purity. But the Blacks did the 'cutting down' themselves. Once it had arrived at

Fairfield it was refined in the factory and then passed on to dealers. The jury learnt of Black's extravagant lifestyle and his 13 bank and building society accounts. They heard that Laming and the Blacks were regularly in touch using walkie-talkies to organise cocaine pick-ups. Some calls lasted no more than 11 seconds, just long enough to arrange a meeting. Walkie-talkies and scanner machines were tuned to police radio frequencies.

During the four-week trial nothing in court was more remarkable than the sensational defence put up by James Laming. Yes, he admitted, he had had meetings with Rene Black. They had made phone calls to each other. But it had nothing to do with drugs. He knew nothing about the drugs laboratory at Fairfield. He denied that he intended to sell the half kilo of cocaine found in his possession. Both Laming and Martin Cox maintained that their link with Black was related to horseracing. They claimed that they had been plotting to subvert horserace betting by using a stun gun on certain horses and that Black supported this project.

Horses, Laming knew, had very sensitive hearing. He told the court that he had obtained a knowledge of ultrasonics from the *Encyclopaedia Britannica* and had mentioned to Black how a stun gun could be used to 'nobble' horses. When Black paid him £10,000 and asked him to provide him with one, Laming had gone to a friend and asked him to make the gun. Laming claimed that the gun was used with some success at Royal Ascot in June

The homes of the Black brothers.

1988 when it caused Greville Starkey's mount, Ile de Chypre, to stumble and throw its rider while leading the field during the George V Handicap.

Not unnaturally this was disputed by the prosecution. There was no doubt that the horse was stopped in its tracks at this meeting but there was certainly no proof that it had been because of the use of a stun gun. This tall story, the prosecution maintained, was being introduced as a diversion. A witness, however, 22 year old Gary Lodge, an electrical appliance maker, told how he had been approached by Laming whom he had known for years and asked to make such a gun disguised as a pair of binoculars and which produced a noise inaudible to humans. Laming had not specified precisely what he intended to do with the gun. Lodge said that he was unaware that it was to be used to halt horses during races.

But Laming's account of his relationship with Black and his denial of all knowledge of Black's drugs empire did not convince the jury. After all when arrested had he not been in possession of a half kilo of cocaine?

The stun gun story was rejected; there was no proof that it was responsible for Ile de Chypre's throwing her rider. The police had argued, in fact, that the high-tech gun was never thought of until Laming was arrested and tucked away in Brixton where he got the idea from a novel entitled *The Jericho Gun*. The jury felt it to be merely a smokescreen to attempt to conceal his drug dealing activities with the Blacks. Laming had claimed that his meetings with the brothers in fields in Surrey were to test the gun on horses but the jury believed that these were the occasions on which cocaine, up to £10 million in value, was handed over.

Passing sentence, the judge commented, 'No doubt you were only one of a number who took part in the supply of cocaine from Black. But even looked at in that way, it is a most serious matter.'

Laming was jailed for 14 years for his part in the drugs conspiracy, with another nine years to run concurrently for possession. Assets of £24,000 were ordered to be seized. In default Laming would serve a further 18 months in jail.

Patrick Fraser was given eight years for possessing a half kilo of cocaine with intent to supply. Assets of £36,000 were ordered to be confiscated, with an additional 18 months in the event of non-payment. It was accepted by the court, however, that Fraser was unaware of the existence of the factory and that he was not part of the conspiracy to flood Britain with cocaine.

Ronald Fisher, Black's father-in-law, who lived at Fairview was given 30 months. He admitted suspecting that sums of money he had helped to launder were from drug trafficking. He was acquitted of a charge of conspiring to produce cocaine.

Martin Cox, the 'betting brain' in the horseracing plot, was cleared of any involvement in the drugs conspiracy.

After the trial was over and prior to sentencing him, Mr Justice Butler observed that he had reduced Black's sentence because of his cooperation with the police, adding: 'You have benefited from drugs trafficking in a sum in excess of £2 million. You were one of those at the centre of the chain of importation, production, and supply of the drug. There must be passed in your case a sentence of imprisonment of substantial length.' Black was then sentenced to 15 years' imprisonment.

The prosecution had pressed for all of Black's drugs assets, assessed at more than £3 million, to be confiscated by the court under the Drug Trafficking Offences Act. The £400,000 found at the Sure Store warehouse near Heathrow had been placed on deposit and already by the time of the trial had accrued significant interest. Black, trying to hang on to some of his gains, claimed that he had made no more than £900,000 from his activities but ultimately the judge ordered that his realisable assets of £1.5 million be confiscated. In the event of non-payment a further 10 years would be added to the sentence. The judge also recommended that on release Black should be deported to Peru.

The end of the Black regime was a massive triumph for NDIU and for Surrey Police working together. For a time it halted the flow of cocaine into the country. The heavy sentences on Rene Black, James Laming and Patrick Fraser were intended to send a warning to others.

But the stun gun? What about that? Despite Laming's story being rejected at Southwark Crown Court, it does seem likely from what Lodge said and from the involvement of Martin Cox, the so-called 'betting brain', that there was a sub-plot connected to racing that involved Laming – and possibly the Blacks. But at the time this was not allowed to get in the way of the principal narrative.

Laming was to reappear in 1999 making high class counterfeit coins at Heybridge in Essex. 'I was aiming for a perfect, faultless coin, same as the mint,' the very talented Mr Laming told the court prior to being sent down for another 18 months.

As for Rudi, who had so fortunately been out of the country at the time of his brother's arrest, he has still not come before a British court. Perhaps, tucked away in some corner of South America, he is still plying his trade.

Since the departure of the Black brothers from England, other empires have risen. There is always someone to inherit such territories – and doubtless they are still active somewhere. The war goes on.

DOING A BERTIE

———————❖———————

You wouldn't recognise Bertie these days. He's surely changed in the last 30 years. And of course the plastic surgery must have helped. Maybe he doesn't have the Zapata-style moustache now either. And they gave him a new identity as well, a new name, a longer one. 'It's got three more letters to it,' Bertie said.

Last heard of, he was living away from his old haunts. He was somewhere north of London – maybe Bedfordshire or Herts, somewhere like that, one of those quieter places. Funny to think about it, Bertie in the country, him being a real town boy. Of course, he may not still be there. Who can say? Maybe he's a respectable old gent now. Maybe his neighbours take him for a retired businessman. They probably don't recognise his naturally violent disposition. But where he is, well, that's anyone's guess.

And you really wonder what sort of life he's living these days. Can't be like the old days, surely. They say that in a year or so after the trial he spent – 'squandered' is the word the *Daily Express* used – between £250,000 and £300,000. (This is equivalent in today's values to around £1.7 million. Similar comparative figures are included throughout the chapter.) The money all went on gambling, alcohol and, inevitably, the ladies, they said, but Bertie is unlikely not to have given some thought to his future. He must have tucked some of it away. Part of the deal had been that he would not lose the proceeds of all his earlier activities and he probably had – ironic, this is – a share of some of the reward money from the banks and the insurance companies. He only wrote that stuff for the newspapers, he said, because he was short of cash and needed the £10,000 (£75,000). And that wouldn't go far with big-spending Bertie. But you begin to wonder if some of the cash was going to the families of some of those whom he had been instrumental in sending down ... as a kind of insurance against a contract killer. Apparently there was a contract out on Bertie at this time, estimated to be as much as £³/₄ million at today's prices.

So is he in a big house now? Has he a place today like the one he had in Selsdon? That was very grand, what you might call 'executive', with impressive gates and a fancy front door and Lord knows how many rooms. And he drove a Lotus. And he employed an au pair. Because Bertie had a kind of style.

You might have called him vulgar. You might have had no time for someone so fat and unfit, someone who reeked of after-shave and whose wrists jangled with gold bracelets and whose fingers were perhaps just too well manicured. You might have thought him a trifle flash. And you might have even disapproved of the quantities of booze he put away. But that was Bertie Smalls, that was the way he was whether you met him in Soho or in Selsdon, or at the club he owned in town or when you saw him down at his property on the Costa del Sol. That was Bertie when he was relaxing. That was Bertie when he wasn't at work, holding up banks.

Because Derek Creighton Smalls – where the 'Bertie' comes from is a mystery – was without any doubt this country's most successful bank robber, leader of the most violent robbery organisation this country has known. He was behind the majority of the major bank robberies of the late Sixties and early Seventies, committing crimes that involved more money than the Great Train Robbery. And then he became better known as the first of the supergrasses.

For over twenty years he had followed his occupation as a robber seriously, expressing his choice philosophically. 'You see we weren't interested in 40 quid a week and a chronic overdraft at the bank,' he told the *Express* later. 'We wanted a few grand under the mattress and a few hundred in the pocket and all that went with that. And if the alternative was a stretch or a bullet in the back – well, that was the name of the game, wasn't it?'

So having made the decision to be a bank robber he began to run the most celebrated robbery teams in London. Banks and jewellers are said to have lost over £3 million (£25 million) from raids organised by Bertie. When the teams he assembled first became active, the police had no idea of their identities but because they

The arrest of Bertie Smalls.

had a particular modus operandi, they were named the Crash Bang Gang. One of their earliest successes was the Hatton Garden robbery of 1969 when they escaped with £296,000 (£3 million).

When Barclays bank at Ilford was raided in February 1970 there were nine in the team. Three of the gang went into the bank, one wearing a ginger wig and spectacles, another with a black wig and spectacles. Both of them carried ammonia. The third, wearing a stick-on moustache, was called Salmon. Bertie recalled the occasion. 'Salmon looked like a city gent and he was armed with a sawn-off shotgun. Five of us remained in the van not far from the bank. A man named Short was to block the road in case there was any trouble with the get-away. I had a shotgun and in the van there was a sledgehammer. I also carried a 12 foot ladder to get over the counter, but by the time we got to the bank it was all over and the guards were on the floor. It was not necessary to use the sledgehammer. We just picked up the sacks of money. One shot was fired outside the bank and a shotgun went off accidentally in the van, narrowly missing my foot.'

This robbery was significant because its haul of over £237,000 (£2$^{1}/_{4}$) made it the most successful bank operation of its kind. And its hallmark was noise and violence, typical of Bertie Smalls' teams. They always employed shock tactics, frightening the unsuspecting clerks and customers with their shouts and swearing, their threats and weapons. And it was all over in less than two minutes. 'We'd be out with the money before anybody knew what was happening' and off to the getaway cars, before anyone had collected their senses.

Bertie claimed to be one of the first bank robbers in Britain to carry a sawn-off shotgun. In his view they were safer because whereas some might try to resist robbers wielding pick-axe handles and iron bars they would be more hesitant when faced by guns. With his balaclava topped by a wide-brimmed hat and perhaps sporting sunglasses, Bertie would stand by the door with the gun while his more active gang members would attack the glass security grilles with sledgehammers and then, using ladders, would climb over the counters to collect the money. On some occasions it was enough simply to fire a single shot at the bank ceiling to gain the attention and cooperation of bank staff and customers. Sometimes anyone who attempted to prevent them would be squirted with ammonia.

In May 1972 there was a close call for Bertie after the National Westminster bank at Palmers Green was raided. The number plate of a Jaguar car used in a trial run had been noted by an off-duty police officer and this was traced back to a garage at Tower Bridge in which Bertie had an interest. But again there was not just quite enough to bring a charge against him.

On 10 August 1972 came the robbery at Barclays at Wembley. Security Express guards were delivering new bank notes and collecting a quantity of old ones for storage when six masked men entered with their trademark shouts, curses, threats; using sledgehammers on counters; firing a shot into the ceiling; ordering staff and customers to lie down. The bagged-up old money being collected for storage was grabbed. One armed man stood at the door while the others carried the money out to a waiting van. In two minutes the operation was finished and the team drove off with £138,000 (£1¼ million). Such military precision, in and out in such a short time, so quick and so frightening, meant that few could recall anything very clearly about any of the gang.

But the newly formed Robbery Squad, concentrating on the gang, heard whispers about Bertie's involvement. Hatton Garden, possibly he had been there, and at Lloyds in Bournemouth in September 1970. Must have been him and his team at Palmers Green too. And was that Bertie at Wembley? Was he the one who fired the shot into the ceiling? Was he the one with the shotgun, standing at the door? One witness thought that it might have been him but he couldn't be certain. Then a criminal found with stolen goods offered five names to the police of people that he had heard were at Wembley. And Bertie's was among them.

On the strength of this and other information several men – among them people described variously as company directors, property developers, car dealers and 'of no fixed occupation' – were arrested. Two of them were found to have considerable sums of money in their deed boxes. Bertie, sunning himself at Torremolinos at the time, learned that the police were after him, that they had come down to the Costa del Sol. And he was aggrieved when he found out that some of his friends had already disappeared from the Sunshine Coast without warning him. 'The wife of one of the boys rings and says, "The Yard's here." I say, "Where's the boys?" And she says they've legged it and left me which gave me the hump.'

Bertie managed to evade the police in Spain and made his way back to England. Then, three days before Christmas 1972, Inspector Victor Wilding called at the house in Selsdon. The only person there was Stella Robinson, the au pair. She told them that Bertie was in Northamptonshire, spending Christmas with his brother. Early next morning Bertie, undignified in his underpants, was arrested.

It was all up. The game was over. The police had a fair amount of evidence against him. If it came to a trial there was a chance that he would go away for a very long time. After all, Bertie had already served two prison sentences. Over several weeks he flirted with the Scotland Yard men. He might, he hinted, be willing to help them if they could cut him some slack. 'You can say it was about 60 or 70 per cent self-survival,' Bertie has said. 'I reckoned I might get 20 to 25 years and be an old man when I came out.' He was aggrieved that his plan to escape from custody had been ignored by his former henchmen and at the same time his so-called friends had not properly supported his wife. 'I was let down ... so I felt I owed nobody nothing,' he said.

So we have the first supergrass, Bertie Smalls, offering information to the police not just about the Wembley robbery but about crimes committed by him and others years earlier. He would name names, he told the police, and in return he would not be imprisoned; he would not be asked to give back what he had stolen and in addition he would be able to claim the rewards of approximately £300,000 (£2^{1}/$_{3}$ million) that had been offered by banks and insurance companies. Bertie Smalls' information came at a high price approved of by the Director of Public Prosecutions. His amnesty covered everything, he said, 'except murder and treason and piracy or something ridiculous like that.'

And to help him in his work assisting the police Bertie and his family were given a suite at the Esso Motor Hotel at Wembley, which had 'a water bed and everything'. It was a luxurious hotel. 'I think it was costing £60 (£500) a day for the room alone,' he has said. 'Plus we was ordering up meals, smoked salmon and wine and the lot, and we was eight-handed.' And that makes no mention of his customary daily bottle of vodka. Presumably the police officers guarding him at this time also enjoyed themselves. *Private Eye* reported that Smalls had been swimming in the nude with a female police officer who later retired as a result of the publicity. Bertie claimed not to have any money. He had spent it all, he said, and he had 'perhaps a couple of hundred quid' left. He was allowed £25 (£300) a week maintenance for himself and family in addition to the free accommodation.

Then came the stories, the full accounts, the details which would strengthen the Crown case against 27 named individuals, Bertie's former friends. A statement of 65 pages included specific details of more than 20 major robberies, including 15 in which he had participated.

More arrests followed.

And eventually Bertie had to stand up in court. He described the committal proceedings held before magistrates in a gymnasium in Wembley: 'There wasn't no court house big enough what with about 27 of them there, each one handcuffed to a copper and about 50 briefs and court officials and all.'

And what an uproar when Bertie went into the witness box to testify against his former team. 'Well, they starts shouting and cursing and saying, "Get over here, Smalls, you belong on this side." And the language was shocking. They kept on singing and making up songs about me. One of the geezers shouts, "You ******** grass", and this is a bloke who grassed on me a few years ago so I'd let him have a mouthful back ... Some I didn't give a damn about, some I know would have done it on me if they'd had the gall. But some were good pals and I liked them and I wouldn't have done it on them for the world except that I had to because the story wouldn't have made sense if I'd left them out. And believe me, it had to make sense.'

And so against a background of such interruptions – the accused sang or hummed *Whispering Green Grass* and *We'll Meet Again* – Bertie testified. According to some who were there in the heavily armed courtroom, what seemed to stiffen Bertie's resolve was a remark by one of the accused about his wife Diane, who was sometime known as Alice. Danny Allpress, one of Bertie's former close friends, whispered loudly across the dock, 'Well, Bertie, who's been having Slack Alice while you're away?' The others in the dock laughed but some saw this as the point where any doubts that Bertie had about testifying dissipated.

At three trials at the Old Bailey during 1974, in courtrooms packed with uniformed and plainclothes policemen, many of whom were armed, 27 defendants, some of London's most ruthless armed robbers, faced 49 charges relating to 20 armed raids between October 1968 and August 1972.

Despite their share in many of the most lucrative bank robberies, a few of these men had exhausted most of their gains in high living. Some were described as unemployed. Others on the other hand had prospered, investing wisely. Some had bought properties in Spain from where Brian Turner, a company director, was extradited. David Lyle was dealing in cars in Poole. Philip Morris, who was also tried on a charge of manslaughter in the course of a robbery at the United Dairies depot at Ewell in February 1973, was arrested at his farm in Cornwall. Thomas French, the former Hayes taxi driver who used to ferry Bertie's gang and their guns to their various assignments, was also picked up at his farm in Cornwall. Then there was company director/property developer Bruce Brown, a close acquaintance of a very senior police officer with whom he had talked only recently about their jointly opening a club in Hounslow. Such was their friendship that Brown had attended the party to celebrate the policeman's most recent step up the ranks. Both men were members of Ashford Manor Golf Club in Middlesex where Brown was captain.

The juries at the separate trials heard about the Hatton Garden and Ilford and Wembley jobs. They heard about Ed Holt, the Wembley bank clerk and part-time disc jockey, who was promised £10,000 (£75,000) for giving vital information about the bank's routines and three dates on which security guards would arrive to take away huge batches of old notes. They heard about Susan Mattis's 'flop' in Hornsea where on one occasion, when preparing for the job at Lloyds in Stoke Newington, a gun carelessly fired blew a hole in her floor. They heard about squaring security guards. And they heard about Bertie who at six o'clock in the morning would prime himself for 'a job' with vodka and grapefruit juice.

In the witness box the 36 year old Bertie Smalls agreed that his record went back to 1958. The charges included possessing an offensive weapon and a firearm, loitering with intent to steal and living off prostitutes. He admitted to having taken part in between 15 and 20 robberies. During his two days in the witness box, he named the men who had joined him in some of the biggest bank raids in London. Was he one of Britain's most successful bank robbers? 'I have done a few,' he answered and there is almost a hint of false modesty about that reply.

'Do you agree', asked Jeremy Hutchison QC, acting for one of the defendants, 'that your success was based on terror and violence?'

Would he explain what he meant, Bertie asked, as though the matter was something he had not previously given much thought to.

'I mean that you succeeded in all these robberies because you put people into a state of terror?'

'We all did,' Bertie replied.

'And having committed them you had the wit to avoid prosecution by the police year after year?'

'You can say that.' And here Bertie seems quite unperturbed, quite matter of fact.

'And now you are doing just the same thing in the witness box?'

'What do you mean?'

'Avoiding prosecution by naming other people and agreeing to give evidence against them in order to escape the just sentence you deserve?'

'You can say that.'

'Not caring who you trample down on the way?'

'I have told you the truth.'

And on this occasion he *was* telling the truth. Bertie Smalls was a man of the worst possible character, a man with an appalling criminal record, a man who had a motive to lie his way out of trouble. But he was not lying when he stood up in the Old Bailey and denounced his former colleagues. As a consequence of his cooperation with the police the 27 defendants were given a total of 322 years. Some received sentences of up to 21 years. One of them, Donald Barrett, who had already received 12 years for the Bournemouth bank robbery, was given another 17 years which was reduced to 12 on appeal. Leonard Jones who had taken part in the Barclays bank robbery at Acton was given 14 years. French, the Hayes taxi driver, was given nine years and Danny Allpress, another car dealer, was given 21 years, reduced on appeal to 18 years.

So they all went to prison and Bertie, the first supergrass, walked away from it all scot-free. Not back to the classy house in Selsdon. But probably to somewhere very nice. After this he kept his head down. Today he may be known as the quiet old chap down the road who tends his garden or the feller always ready to pass the time of day in the village local. He can never speak of the good old days when he was a top man at his trade, can't talk about the buzz, the thrill of it all, the meticulous planning, the things that went wrong as well as those that worked. Bertie Smalls can't stand up in the pub and boast that he was the man who immediately reduced bank robberies in London by 60 per cent. He can't tell his listeners that it was all because of him that the banks began to adopt more stringent procedures to protect themselves; because of him the Robbery Squad was formed with a specialist interest in major crimes; he can't boast that because of him some of the best thieves in London were tucked away in Durham and Strangeways, Dartmoor and Wandsworth; he can't claim that because of him more criminals facing severe sentences decided to turn supergrass.

But the supergrass was never popular, not even with the Law. Considering the appeals of some of those convicted, Lord Justice Lawton was not impressed by the idea. To him Bertie was 'a craven villain'. 'The spectacle of the Director of Public Prosecutions recording in writing, at the behest of a criminal like Smalls, his undertaking to give immunity from further prosecution, is one which we find distasteful,' Lord Lawton said. 'Nothing of a similar kind must ever happen again. Undertakings of immunity from prosecution may have to be given in the public interest. They should never be given by the police. The Director should give them most sparingly and, in cases involving grave crimes, it would be prudent of him to consult the law officers before making any promises.'

Today supergrasses are not offered the privileges that Bertie Smalls enjoyed at Wembley. There are no more luxury hotels, no long conjugal visits, no more alcohol. Though Bertie's contribution to cutting crime was successful, the use of supergrasses later led to collapsed trials, acquittals and successful appeals. The system is certainly open to abuse. But for a time use of the supergrass was effective. 'Faced with trustworthy detectives for the first time in their experience,' according to Sir Robert Mark, the Metropolitan Police Commissioner, 'organised criminals began to sing.'

Donald Barrett, whose long sentences were to lead to his becoming a supergrass himself, has commented rather whimsically, 'They should have put a bullet in the first one's nut. That would have stopped it in its tracks.' Perhaps it would.

And perhaps the expression 'Doing a Bertie' would never have become a common expression in certain communities.

Brinkley Goes to Croydon

❁

So on the Saturday Brinkley takes the train to Croydon. Something's got to be done about Parker. Everything's getting just too difficult and if Parker goes and tells the Probate Court about signing the papers, that will be the end for Brinkley. They'll look into matters and Brinkley will lose all that he has so recently gained. The house, the furnishings, the money in the bank – he'll lose it all. So it's a case of Brinkley or Parker.

And Parker will be waiting with the dog, thinking that is what Brinkley's coming down about. Brinkley wrote to him a couple of days earlier saying he was desperate to buy a guard dog. Burglars had been trying to get into the house next door, he said, and he wanted to make sure they didn't pay him a visit. So he wanted a really vicious dog, maybe a bulldog, he'd told Parker in the letter and he'd come down on the Saturday to collect it. And he'd pay Parker in chickens, Brinkley said, knowing that he did some dealing in fowl of various kinds.

Anyway, here comes Richard Brinkley, tall and rather thin with a long, skinny neck but, for all that, still a good-looking chap even though he is 53 years old. He has a strong, characterful sort of face, his nose rather hawk-like and his eyes sharp and glittery. His hair is thinning now but it's still black, not a hint of grey, just like his moustache but, if truth be told, Mr Brinkley does use dye at times. And he is, you have to say, a bit of a charmer, the sort of man who makes the best of himself. And he makes his way to Parker's lodgings at 32 Churchill Road.

But he has an errand first. He'll take Parker a bottle of oatmeal stout, just as a kind of friendly gift. It'll go down nicely along with the prussic acid he has in his pocket. Poisoning – that is Richard Brinkley's intention this April evening of 1907. He's out to poison Reginald Parker, an acquaintance – no more than that – for the last couple of years, but who now is likely to come up with information in court that could send Brinkley to prison for a long time. Perhaps, in fact, if there was too much probing into his background he might be sent to the gallows. So Brinkley, on his way to meet this acquaintance of his, calls in at Hardstone's off-licence in Brighton Road, only minutes away from where Parker lodges. As for the dog, well, Brinkley doesn't really want one but he has to make up some excuse for seeing Parker.

When Brinkley arrives at the house, sometime after 8.15 pm, he finds Parker already supping a couple of bottles of ale with his landlord, Richard Beck, like Brinkley a carpenter by trade. Brinkley produces his own bottle with a flourish. 'The doctor's advised me to drink stout,' he tells the others. But their glasses are already full and they don't want the stout. Still, they chat agreeably, the three men, before Beck says he has to go out to meet his wife and daughters. And then Brinkley and Parker discuss the dog, which is tied by its lead to the door of the sitting room. Brinkley says he's certainly very pleased with the animal because it looks ferocious enough to frighten off any burglars but he doesn't want to take it off home to Fulham himself. Perhaps Parker will bring it the next day. So they decide that the following morning Parker will bring it to Brinkley's house. They sip their drinks and then Brinkley asks for a glass of water. Parker understands why: Brinkley is a teetotaller and he doesn't like the taste of the stuff so he has taken only a couple of sips. Off goes Parker into the kitchen to fetch the water. It's the opportunity that Brinkley has been waiting for. He pours the prussic acid into the bottle.

But isn't it just how things turn out in life? You make your plans and people simply let you down. And in this case no matter how frequently Brinkley proffers the stout – 'Go on, try it, you'll like it' – Parker will not have so much as a sip. And finally Brinkley has to go. Time to get the train back to Fulham. And instead of Parker staying behind in the house he comes out with his visitor. He's going to visit a friend now, he says, and he'll not be back at

Richard Brinkley.

Churchill Road till later. So they part outside the house. And Brinkley resolves that when Parker comes with the dog on the next day he will not escape so easily, because time is pressing.

So the house is left empty, save for the dog. And the bottle of oatmeal stout, almost untouched, stands on the table of the sitting room.

But the following day Parker didn't turn up at Brinkley's house. He was in fact being questioned about the murder of his landlord, his landlord's wife and possibly – it was a matter of touch and go – his landlord's daughter. For later on the Saturday night, at nearly 11 o'clock, Richard and Elizabeth Beck with their 21 year old elder daughter Daisy had returned home. They sat down by the sitting room fire.

And there on the table was the bottle of oatmeal stout. Beck poured himself a glass and offered his wife a taste. But she took only the slightest sip and pulled a face and spat it out into the fire. It was horrible, she said, far too bitter. And Daisy, taking only a tentative sip, felt the same about it. 'Oh, how bitter it is!' she said. But her father dismissed the women's complaints. They didn't know what was good for them, he told them, swallowing the rest of the glass. Barely had he emptied the glass than he fell to the floor, foaming at the mouth, gasping for breath, his body convulsed. Then both women were similarly affected.

When 17 year old Hilda Beck came in shortly afterwards she found her parents and sister on the floor. She immediately ran to the neighbours' houses seeking help and they sent for a doctor but by the time he arrived both father and mother were beyond aid. Only Daisy showed the faintest signs of life and she was shortly removed to hospital where for days she lingered between life and death. Gradually she made a recovery.

Early on Sunday, 21 April, Parker was called in for questioning. After all, it seemed quite obvious. It must be the lodger. Who could possibly think that he was not guilty? But then he told them about Brinkley and how he had been to the house and had brought a bottle of stout with him.

Chief Inspector Fowler of Scotland Yard then picked up Brinkley. 'Well, I'm sugared,' he exclaimed when the detective spoke to him. 'I wasn't at Croydon last night. Well, I'm sugared. This is awkward, ain't it?' he went on, blustering his innocence. 'Does Parker say I done it?' he asked. 'They won't believe him. He's a dirty bloody tyke and spiteful towards every one. I am a good character and a teetotaller. And if anyone says I've bought beer,' he said indignantly, 'they have got to prove it.'

But at that point nobody but Brinkley had mentioned beer.

When the remains of the bottle of stout were analysed it was found to contain a heavy dosage of prussic acid, the poison that acts like a fatal stroke of lightning.

Brinkley was charged with murder.

And then there were further investigations, the magistrates' courts and the trial at Guildford Assizes, which revealed a complex tale of obsessive greed and a murderous mind.

For the past eight or nine years Richard Brinkley had been friendly with a German widow, Johanna Maria Blume, whom he visited regularly. It seems to have been an affectionate relationship with no sexual undertones. Mrs Blume was in fact 25 years older than Brinkley who cheerfully called her 'Granny'.

It is difficult to get behind this relationship. Admittedly Mrs Blume was comfortably off. She had her own well-furnished home in Fulham and, at today's values, about £50,000 in the bank. Certainly Brinkley was keen on money and as a carpenter he did not earn significant sums. There is no evidence for this – but was he sponging off the old lady all these years? What other reasons were there for such assiduous attention to the widow? But these questions must remain unanswered.

On 19 December 1906 the old lady died suddenly. Her granddaughter, 21 year old Augusta Glanville, an actress then appearing in panto at Fulham and who lived with her, left Mrs Blume that evening in good health but only an hour or so later she was found dead. Well, nothing suspicious there. Old people do die without warning.

As her death was so sudden there was an inquest. The coroner, Mr Ingleby Oddie, was to write later, 'I ordered a post-mortem examination which did not reveal any disease. But in the brain there were some small haemorrhages which her doctor, with some little hesitation, declared were apoplectic in nature and were the cause of death. Deaths from apoplexy which takes place as quickly as this – that is, within an hour – are almost invariably due to very large haemorrhages in the brain. And as those found in this case were quite small, I did not feel too satisfied about this death. One would hardly expect a few tiny haemorrhages on the surface of the brain to cause death so quickly.'

So in the court were Mrs Blume's doctor, who spoke 'with some little hesitation', and Ingleby Oddie who 'did not feel too satisfied about the death'. But neither was of the opinion that there could be anything really suspicious about the matter. 'In the absence of any other cause of death, and on the assurance of the doctor who performed the post-mortem examination that the death was a natural one,' Ingleby Oddie wrote, 'the jury, under my direction, recorded a verdict of natural death from cerebral haemorrhage – that is to say, from apoplexy.'

And that might have been expected to be the end of the affair. Alas, it was simply the beginning.

A day or two after the inquest, Brinkley called at Mrs Blume's Fulham house, announcing that he was 'master here'. To prove his claim he produced a document which he asserted was Mrs Blume's will. Caroline Glanville, her daughter, suddenly aware that the home she had assumed her mother to be leaving her was no longer to be hers, demanded to inspect the document. And there it was, signed by the old lady. And there was no mistake about it. There was the old lady's signature with the accompanying signatures of two witnesses. Everything, house, contents, jewellery, money – all now belonged to Brinkley.

Within days, Brinkley took occupation of the house. Caroline and Augusta were obliged to find other accommodation but were wise enough to consult a solicitor. After all, no one had even suspected that the old lady would nominate Brinkley as her exclusive heir. The solicitor then entered a caveat against the will which appeared to have been signed only two days before Mrs Blume's death. It was now incumbent upon Brinkley to prove the validity of the will.

In the meantime Brinkley had begun pawning various items of furniture. He must have felt very secure about his position. When, however, he heard about the legal action, he was inevitably concerned. One sentence in the solicitor's letter was particularly disturbing. 'We would like to talk to the witnesses,' it said.

Brinkley's first strategy was to visit Caroline. In fact he called on her twice, each time offering to marry her provided the solicitor dropped proceedings. It was after all her mother's wish that they should marry, he told her. It was the first time that Caroline had heard that.

That the witnesses to the will were to be brought before the court alarmed Brinkley for the document was forged and Parker in particular rather than Heard, the other signatory, presented a great threat. Parker could say precisely how he had been tricked into signing the will. He would swear that he had never met Mrs Blume, that he had never knowingly signed a will but that he vaguely recalled signing another paper.

Parker comes over as a not especially sharp man. At the time his life was in some turmoil as he had recently separated from his wife and he was also on the verge of bankruptcy. Since the previous December he had been ill and the doctor had diagnosed depression. There was even some fear that he might commit suicide. He was a financially desperate accountant, if you can believe that such a creature exists. This may be why he supplemented his income dealing in livestock and dogs.

In late 1906 – and this was before Mrs Blume's death and seven or eight months before the Becks' poisoning the following year – Brinkley had asked Parker to draw up a draft will. He probably explained that he was really not much of a pen man, not a good speller and not well acquainted with such matters. He was only a jobbing carpenter after all, was probably how Brinkley put it. So Parker drew up a will in the most general terms. There were few specific details in the document save for a reference to some stocks and shares and a Post Office Savings Bank account. It would be not unreasonable for Parker to assume that Brinkley was on the point of putting his own affairs in order. But Parker did not sign the document immediately.

At about the same time Parker was asked to draw up another document for Brinkley who said he was arranging a charabanc trip to the seaside. Should be fun – high jinks, eh? It was a simple enough document. All it required were some headings – name, address, pick-up point, that sort of thing. No difficulty for Parker and no doubt Brinkley said how he admired Parker's skill with the pen.

On 19 December, late at night, only a couple of hours or so after Mrs Blume's death, Brinkley met Parker and asked him if he would be going on the outing. If so would he sign up? Parker must have scarcely glanced at it as he signed his name. And would he sign a second copy, he was asked. For the records. Parker duly complied, not considering it odd that the paper was tightly folded and not noticing that it was dated two days earlier. Parker had signed the bogus will.

But now, months later, the plan was falling apart. And in court Parker would talk about the will he had drawn up and the outing paper and the fact that he had been tricked into signing them. It would be all up for Brinkley unless he silenced Parker. And so began the round of murder attempts that ended up with the deaths of the Becks.

Many students of this case have said that Parker was aware that Brinkley tried on three occasions to poison him. But can he really have suspected this? Was there really a cat and mouse game being played? It is difficult to believe. And, anyway, in court Parker stated categorically that he was unaware that Brinkley was trying to poison him.

One evening in March Parker visited Brinkley at Fulham and was surprised to be offered whisky by a confirmed teetotaller. It is likely that this was an attempt at murder, but Parker did not like whisky and, rather than offend his host, he threw his drink in the fireplace during Brinkley's brief absence. He then stayed on to eat lamb chops prepared by Brinkley. Presumably the blundering poisoner assumed that Parker had swallowed the poison.

Another evening in the same month Brinkley visited Parker who was then in 'digs' in South Norwood. On this occasion Brinkley is said to have attempted to poison Parker's cup of tea. Parker recalled the occasion: that was the night he just did not drink his cup of tea but left it to get cold.

Parker has been represented as a man who kept his eye on the man he knew was trying to poison him. Is it likely? Would he constantly keep in touch with a man out to murder him?

And so to the Croydon meeting when Brinkley went to Parker's new lodgings at 32 Churchill Road, ostensibly to collect his guard dog. But Brinkley found the wrong victims. Within days he was charged with the murder of the Becks.

Unsurprisingly Mrs Blume's body was now exhumed but no charge was ever made against the prisoner in connection with her death. Sir Bernard Spilsbury conducted the post mortem and sent off certain organs for analysis. However, there was no hint of prussic acid although some traces of arsenic were discovered. So small was the amount that it could not be proved as the cause of death. But had Mrs Blume been poisoned with prussic acid there would have been no sign of this either after five months' burial, for cyanides are quickly altered by metabolic activity once they enter the body.

As far as Mrs Blume's death was concerned, on the face of it Brinkley was innocent. Nevertheless there must be some doubts. Perhaps the best that can be said for him is that the murder of the old lady could not be proved.

Throughout this period, as he awaited trial, Brinkley was optimistic that he would be found innocent of murder. His

Brinkley in court.

argument was that he had not intended to poison the Becks. They had died solely because they had taken a drink not intended for them.

Brinkley was tried at Guildford Assizes before Mr Justice Bigham, charged with murdering the Becks and attempting to murder Daisy Beck and Reginald Parker. He was to bluster his way through the trial, claiming not to have been in Croydon on the night of the Becks' death. Indeed, he said that he had never been there and that on the night in question he was in the King's Road, Chelsea. He was, however, never able to confirm this alibi.

Brinkley's hopes must have risen when the Brighton Road licensee failed to recognise him at an identity parade but that was possibly because overnight his moustache had changed colour from black to grey, the effect of washing away the dye he used. On the other hand she did recall that on that evening a customer, with a general likeness to Brinkley, had bought a bottle of oatmeal stout. She remembered him because at first he had refused to pay the twopence deposit on the bottle and had then insisted that the bottle should be stamped with the address of the off-licence so that there should be no shilly-shallying about returning the deposit. (Our great murderers have often revealed similar mean streaks. One recalls George Joseph Smith who quibbled about the price of the portable bath he intended to drown one of his brides in. Then there was Frederick Seddon who poisoned his lodger and then arranged for her burial in a common grave. He was paid commission by the undertaker for introducing the business.) But it was a shop lad who was able to point out Brinkley as having been in the shop that night.

And then a railway inspector who knew Brinkley was to tell the court that he had seen him catch a train from Chelsea to Croydon on the Saturday evening.

William Vale, a veterinary surgeon in South Norwood, was another witness who put paid to Brinkley's pleas of innocence. He had consulted his poisons register and said that on 19 June 1906 Brinkley had asked for poison to kill a dog. Vale had sold him prussic acid but then Brinkley had gone back saying that he had spilt it. Could he have some more? Vale had given him a second quantity.

Brinkley's claims that he had not seen Parker for three weeks before the murders, his astonishment that Parker should lie about him, cut little ice with the court although Brinkley stoutly defended himself and continued throughout to maintain his innocence. But the prosecution hounded him about his knowledge of poison. Had he ever studied it, he was asked. What did he know about the qualities of prussic acid? What about a document in his possession that described the reactions of water on nitrate of silver? Why should he have such a document? His answers were not convincing.

In the dock Brinkley burst into tears at the mention of Mrs Blume. He claimed that Parker was lying: he had definitely signed the will in the presence of the old lady. Another man, Herbert Heard, had actually drawn up the will and signed it. He could prove that Parker had signed the will. But Heard was never called to give evidence and certain conclusions may be drawn from this.

Parker, in the witness box, explained that he had known Brinkley for two years. He said he had never witnessed a will though he admitted that he had signed a paper of some kind. One handwriting expert pointed out that the signature of Mrs Blume on the will was different from some receipts that were undeniably in her handwriting. This was the first occasion on which handwriting experts gave testimony in a murder case.

After a jury withdrawal for 55 minutes Brinkley was found guilty of the murder of the Becks.

A correct verdict? Jurists quibbled at the time. It did present a nice legal conundrum. Was it right to find him guilty of murder when he had intended no harm to the people who had died? Should their deaths be regarded as accidental? Today, the law might come to a different conclusion.

From his cell, still protesting his innocence, Brinkley wrote, 'I do appeal for mercy from the capital charge until the mystery that surrounds these poor people's deaths is cleared. Whether they committed suicide or not I cannot tell. I wish I could, but I believe I could if I had time.'

In a moment of gratitude he wrote, 'I give to Walter Frampton, Esquire, of the Middle Temple, London, barrister at law, all my masonic regalia as a memento for the able manner in which he defended me on my recent trial.'

And then came a remarkable bequest. 'I bequeath all my real and personal estate to my trustee upon trust for the Royal Masonic Institution for Girls.' This, perhaps unsurprisingly, was rejected.

Brinkley was executed at Wandsworth on 13 August 1907.

And that ought to be the end of Brinkley's story. In a sense it is. But there was a beginning too which ought not to be neglected.

Years before Mrs Blume and Parker and the Becks came on the scene, back in the 1880s, Margaret Stone, a farmer's daughter from Hertfordshire, fell in love with Sir Richard Bradley, who was conducting chemical experiments on local soil. She ran away to live with him in London. When she found out he was not a knight nor a Bradley nor, come to that, a soil chemist, she stayed with him, her carpenter, her Brinkley. She never seems to have queried the large black case with its three bottles of chemicals.

And then one day the landlady found Mrs Brinkley – they'd never married but there were decencies to observe – dead on the sitting room sofa. And there were the poisons: prussic acid, strychnine, arsenic, ergot of rye and chloroform. And she had died of arsenic poisoning.

The jury brought in a case of suicide. As to the poisons, Brinkley explained these were used in his 'electrical and photographic experiments'.

A year or so later, after coming out of prison, having served seven months for stealing bicycles, Brinkley, calling himself William Ridgley, met a 17 year old, Laura Glenn. She too was to take arsenic in Brinkley's rooms, leaving a suicide note to her beloved who had, she declared, broken her heart.

Then a wife who gave birth to a son and daughter died suddenly of heart failure. There is no indication of how this came about.

Of course no one ever said that these women were murdered. Make what you will of the matter.

WINDOW OF OPPORTUNITY

---❀---

The upstairs-downstairs world which existed for centuries and which has now all but disintegrated was based on class, sustained by wealth and not infrequently by a mutual trust, affection and loyalty. And yes, at times there was thoughtless cruelty or indifference on the one hand just as on the other there was contempt and dishonesty. In the great town houses and in the imposing country seats of the aristocracy huge dramas were acted out in sculleries and kitchens of which those upstairs in the libraries and the dining rooms knew nothing. Similarly, over port and cigars, or with the Earl Grey and cucumber sandwiches, lurid gossip and heart-rending tragedies were whispered about – not of course in front of the servants, though these latter often knew more of the private worlds of their masters and mistresses than they would admit. But this is where the trust came in. The great lords and their ladies expected loyalty and discretion from the lower orders. What is undeniable is that their expectations were generally realised.

It was greatly to the credit of the sixth Duke and Duchess of Sutherland that they recognised their responsibilities to the wider society and at Sutton Place, that great and glorious Tudor house near Guildford, they regularly employed among their kitchen and pantry staff boys who had been released from approved schools. The Duchess would always maintain that given a chance, treated fairly, and with realistic expectations placed upon them, the boys would turn out well. It was not the ex-Borstal boys who let the Sutherlands down in November 1950: it was others in senior positions of trust.

At this time Sutton Place, which had been greatly modernised by the Sutherlands, was on the point of being sold to Paul Getty, the American oil tycoon. The house was gradually being emptied of its magnificent furnishings and its great pictures, its library of books and all of the personal treasures handed down through the generations. It was no longer a comfortable home to be in and so the Duke and Duchess moved into Gardens Cottage, which was, despite its rather modest name, a substantial house in the beautifully manicured parkland of the estate. They aimed to stay there for a few days before returning to their London home.

On the night of 4 November, as the Duchess was preparing for bed she saw that the bedroom window was open and then realised to her horror that two ordinary oak boxes which had been placed in her bedroom were missing. They had contained her jewellery, valued then at £54,000 and at today's estimate as much as £1,100,000. This was a major professional theft.

Among the thirty items stolen were a cultured pearl necklace; a diamond and emerald brooch; two large and two smaller diamond bracelets; a large single stone diamond ring; a diamond brooch; an openwork diamond-bow clip; two smaller clips; a diamond watch-bracelet; an aquamarine bracelet; topaz and diamond earrings and other magnificent pieces.

It was that doyen of Surrey detectives, Tom Roberts (see also 'The Cutt Mill Murder'), who went down to Gardens Cottage. He took statements from staff and set about contacting former employees too. He concluded that the thief had had inside information. Not only had he known exactly where the jewels were but he had known when to climb up his ladder to the bedroom window. He must have known that at the time the Duke and Duchess were playing canasta in the ground floor sitting room. And yet no one among the staff knew about the jewellery except for the lady's-maid and Donald Macleod, the butler.

The 39 year old Macleod was a very strong suspect. It is not axiomatic to assume that 'the butler done it' but who else in the house was as likely? Roberts felt uneasy about the man. He had only recently, in March 1950, joined the Duke's staff and was due to move on to another appointment on 17 November. There was no long-lasting tie of loyalty here. That much was evident. On the other hand Macleod had the highest references. He had worked in positions of trust in other great houses and was now on the point of becoming butler to the ambassador at the Cuban Embassy in Cheyne Walk.

Macleod was interviewed several times by Roberts, but always said that he knew nothing about the theft. No, he had not stolen the jewellery and, no, he had not given anyone any information about where it was in the house. Even after leaving the Duke's employ, Macleod was visited from time to time by Roberts who continued prodding him, suggesting possibilities. But all the time Macleod insisted on his innocence.

Roberts' probing over the months led him to wonder about Victor Sparkes, former valet of the Duke, who had left his post only weeks after the arrival of Macleod at Sutton Place. The Duchess had told Roberts that she had employed Mrs Sparkes as her lady's-maid. While her husband had never had access to the jewels, Mrs Sparkes most certainly had. Could she have told her husband about the jewellery, Roberts wondered.

Further digging by Roberts led him to Albert Burley, a 32 year old Lavender Hill bookmaker. Although Burley had no convictions he was suspected of planning a series of robberies at large country houses and of receiving stolen property. And it transpired that he was a close friend of Sparkes. And since leaving Sutton Place, Sparkes had maintained a relationship with Macleod. The two men met quite regularly. Was this the connection then? The three men conspiring together, working out a plan to steal the jewels, with Macleod the inside man?

But despite his certainty Roberts could not break down Macleod's story. He became convinced that his suspect was afraid of Sparkes and Burley. In some way they had a hold over him. Macleod for his part asked Roberts to stop calling on him. Was this because he was afraid that he would be silenced? Certainly Roberts told Macleod that he was concerned about his safety. Should he ever need to, Macleod must not be afraid to contact him. By patiently maintaining this contact with his evidently frightened prime suspect the policeman hoped that some day his patience would be rewarded.

At the same time pressure was kept up on Burley and Sparkes. Both men were questioned and both repeatedly denied any involvement in the robbery. But they were closely watched over the succeeding 14 months and were subject to extensive enquiries. In the spring of 1951 police discovered that Burley used a safe deposit box in Chancery Lane. Obtaining a warrant, they searched the box and found in it nearly £4,500 in small denomination bank notes but no jewellery. Burley claimed it was money he kept in reserve for his horseracing activities. Sparkes paid visits to France on three occasions and each time customs officers checked to ensure that the jewellery was not being smuggled abroad.

In 1952 Macleod left the Cuban Embassy and went to work for Lord Thorneycroft. The whole matter of the theft had been preying on his mind and no doubt Roberts' persistence caused him further anxiety. Shortly after his appointment, Macleod confessed to his new employer that he had played a part in a burglary of a previous employer. Lord Thorneycroft advised him to go to the Metropolitan Police and when he did they passed him on to Tom Roberts.

Yes, he told the policeman, he had participated in the theft at Sutton Place. Now he wanted to get it off his chest. He would face criminal charges, Roberts warned him, but it seems that Macleod was only too anxious to unburden himself. He told how Sparkes had asked him if he 'could do with some easy money'. And who would not? But what would he have to do? He had always been a law-abiding man. He was uncertain. He wouldn't want to do anything seriously bad. But he was hooked. Sparkes had him on the line. It was then that Sparkes introduced him to Burley, the prime mover in the theft, who asked him for information 'to help them steal my employers' jewels'.

The three men met several times both in London and at Worplesdon, near Guildford. At these meetings Macleod explained the lay-out of Gardens Cottage. Perhaps Sparkes had never been there during his time in service at Sutton Place. He agreed that on the night planned for the robbery he would open the window of the Duchess's bedroom while she and the Duke were at dinner.

On the night of the burglary Burley and Sparkes hid near Gardens Cottage. They were given the all-clear signal by Macleod, who drove a small van from the cottage towards Sutton Place house. To establish his alibi he collected some items from the house. Once Burley and Sparkes saw the van they were able to go ahead. Using a ladder to the upstairs bedroom window, Burley climbed through the window and took the two boxes. Easy.

Over the next twelve months MacLeod was paid a number of small amounts for his part in the robbery. He had, he said, been promised £8,000 but that was later reduced to £1,000. By the time of his confession he had received only about £800.

At the Surrey Quarter Sessions in Kingston in April 1952, in a trial lasting four days, the three men were charged with conspiring together between March and November 1950 in Worplesdon and elsewhere 'unlawfully to break and enter Gardens Cottage, Sutton Place, Guildford, Surrey, and therein feloniously to steal a quantity of jewellery and money valued together at £53,635, the property and monies of the Duke of Sutherland.'

The Director of Public Prosecutions then advised that all charges against Macleod be dropped so that he could appear as the principal prosecution witness. Despite facing a stern cross-examination from the defence, Macleod was absolutely convincing. As prosecuting counsel Mr H.F. Cassells said, 'When Macleod told the truth about the robbery, he could not possibly have known that the charges against him for being concerned would be dropped or stopped. He thought that he would be facing a long term of imprisonment.' That further added to the sincerity of Macleod's testimony.

Perhaps the jury was less convinced by the undeniably suave Victor Sparkes. Tall, dark and handsome, a man of style and swagger, he played his part with élan, arriving at the court each day in a saloon car and accompanied by a French dancer, Mlle Hugette Mony, who was then appearing in a revue, *Peep Show*, at a West End theatre. Great stuff but could you really trust such a chap?

Unsurprisingly, the two accused denied all charges brought against them. Sparkes said that Macleod was lying, that he had a grievance against him because he (Sparkes) had 'enticed' Miss Clemencia Bruno, a young Portuguese cook, away from the Cuban Embassy, where Macleod was working at the time. This was, Sparkes said, all about Macleod being peevish and wanting to get his own back.

Burley did not attribute any such motive to his accuser. He simply claimed that on the night of the theft he was letting off fireworks with his wife and children on Clapham Common.

In the end, Burley was gaoled for seven years and Sparkes for five.

But was Macleod a villain? Certainly the other two can fairly claim such a title but perhaps Macleod was, as Roberts believed, a decent man who once in his lifetime had been tempted and had then deeply regretted his actions. Roberts tended to think that Burley and Sparkes had some hold over Macleod, which was possibly connected to his drinking habits.

After the trial Macleod returned to Lord Thorneycroft's employment. When Thorneycroft became Chancellor of the Exchequer a reporter published the story of Macleod's part in the robbery at Sutton Place. Fearing that this would embarrass his employer Macleod retired and went to live with his sister.

And the jewellery was never recovered. Did Burley and that dashing man about town, Victor Sparkes, come out after serving their time to a nice little nest egg? Most likely they did.

PEANUTS

———————— ❂ ————————

Question: If you offer peanuts who takes the job?
Answer: Somebody who is satisfied to live on peanuts.

There's a moral here somewhere. Something about the labourer being worth his hire. There's no point in expecting high-class, professional work from somebody who is totally unskilled. Stands to reason, doesn't it? You want a good job, you pay for it. Mind you, we need to have a little understanding here. Recruiting for certain jobs is difficult. In certain trades there aren't that many people available and those few are often, for a variety of reasons, difficult to come by. Advertise? Impossible. Think what would happen if you stuck a notice in the small ads asking for 'A contract killer. Discretion essential. Satisfactory references required.'

On the other hand, you might put the word out. You might meet an acquaintance in a pub and hint that you're after someone to do a ticklish sort of job. And he says, putting his finger to his nose and tapping it, he'll ask around. Next thing you know is that you're confiding to a total stranger that you want someone 'taken out', 'rubbed out', 'obliterated'. You're new to this kind of thing. You're not even sure of the right kind of words to use. And it doesn't matter anyway because it turns out that he's an undercover policeman and you're nabbed. So you see, it's difficult even finding someone to do the job.

And then even if you do find a suitable candidate you might not make it worth his while. Contract killers come expensive. At least the good ones do. And if you pay peanuts then you might be storing up trouble for yourself because you might have found yourself an absolute bungler. Just as Alec Bristow did.

Alec Bristow ran GSD Security based in Merstham. And immediately alarm bells ring and question marks pop up all over the place. A security firm boss hiring a killer? And why does he select one who is so eminently incompetent? Men who run security firms ought at least to know that for every Moriarty, for every Napoleon of crime, there are a thousand bunglers. And surely he ought to know that good men come a good deal more expensive than £100 and an old Ford Granada with flat batteries and bald tyres. Not very business-like. From the outset you find you have little faith in the competence of either of these men, Bristow for offering peanuts and his hitman for accepting them.

Bristow had concluded that the only way to overcome a new business rival was to have him shot. That was how things were when one of his employees, his former manager, Dougie Burns, decided to set up a security firm. Alec Bristow's response to the threat of another such firm on the scene was unusual. He might not have liked the idea, but his method of dealing with the prospect of opposition was extreme.

Bristow contacted 41 year old Paul Garfield Jones, an antiques dealer who could perhaps be more accurately described as a career criminal. Jones, living in East Grinstead, was well known to the police, his 'sheet' containing 16 offences going back 26 years. It listed a history of robbery, burglary and firearms offences. And here he was, after so much experience of crime, taking on a killing for so little reward. That Jones was a career criminal cannot be doubted, but it is obvious that he was not terribly successful at his chosen career.

So how did they prepare for the murder of Dougie Burns? What sort of information does a contract killer require before setting out on the job? He needs the name, address and physical description of his target. Perhaps his employer can give him some specific details about his intended victim's habits. What about method? Car accident? Mugging that leads to death? Shooting? Strangling? There are all sorts of possibilities but Jones and Bristow decided that a shooting might be best. What about the district? Burns lived in Hill Crescent, Worcester Park. There were good escape routes by car. All Jones had to do was shoot his man and make his way to where he had parked his car. Shouldn't be too difficult.

Paul Garfield Jones (John Connor Press Associates).

So on 29 November 1999 at about 9.45 pm Jones, the career criminal, limps down Hill Crescent. Limps? Well, he has to conceal the weapon somewhere. You can't wander round Worcester Park with a sawn-off 12-bore shotgun in your hand, no matter what the time of day.

Arriving at the house Jones hesitates, elects to enter the driveway. For a moment or two he pauses by the Volvo that is parked there. What is his plan? That seems very vague. Is he intending to knock on the door and when Burns answers is he going to blast him there and then? And what if his wife opens the door? Will he barge past her and into the house? And if Burns does happen to be in the house where will he be? But supposing he is out ...?

Perhaps it is preoccupations of this kind that lead to his hesitation. His uncertain manner causes him to be spotted by the occupants of the house. Maureen calls out to her husband. Tells him that there's someone hanging around in the driveway. He's wearing dark clothing and something like a hood or a balaclava. Suspicious. Is he after the car? Is he going to break into it? They've had some stealing recently from garden sheds, tools going, lawn mowers, that sort of thing. Is that what the man lurking outside is after? And Jones sees the silhouette through the glass door. Someone coming out. Time to let him have it. But he doesn't. The sawn-off gun is still down his trouser leg. The man comes out of the house and Jones is on his way, back into the roadway, making for his car which he has parked some streets away.

So Jones is off, still limping, but the chap is after him, following him, all the way along Hill Crescent, along Burnham Drive and into Glyn Road. And at last Jones pulls the rifle from his trousers. And as the man gets closer Jones turns round and shoots him once in the stomach. Job done.

Within minutes police and ambulance had arrived. Glyn Road and the surrounding roads were cordoned off and sniffer dogs scoured the area. There were the usual house to house enquiries. But there was no sign of the gunman.

But it was not Dougie Burns lying there on the damp November pavement. Perhaps he was still sitting at home watching television, unaware that he had been targeted, that he had been a candidate for death. In fact it was Ernest Broom, a 57 year old plasterer, who had never had any dealings with Alec Bristow or his security firm. His only link with Bristow was that he lived next door to Dougie Burns. Jones had bungled the job, had failed two of the elementary rules of contract killing: make sure that you know where your target will be; make sure that you shoot the right man. And instead this Johnnie-come-cheaply had endangered another man's life.

Broom had thought that the intruder might be after either his work tools or his gardening equipment and he was determined not to let him get away lightly. He stubbornly – and it has to be said, bravely, for he was no longer a young man – followed the shady looking character along the road. But when he caught up with Jones, 'He did not give me a chance. He just shot me. If I had known he had a gun I would have backed away.'

Fortunately, and thanks to the urgent attentions of the ambulance service and the ministrations of the staff at St Helier Hospital, Broom survived after life-saving surgery. But it can be said that his life since has been severely damaged for he has never worked since. He is permanently disabled. The pellets from Jones's shotgun, which left 250 perforations in the bowel, are still lodged in his stomach. As for Jones and Bristow, they were brought to justice. At Kingston Crown Court in December 2000 Jones was convicted of the attempted murder of Ernest Broom, conspiracy to murder Dougie Burns and possessing a firearm with intent to endanger life. Sentencing Jones to 17 years, Mr Justice Tilling commented: 'Based on the facts of this case and your previous record of a number of convictions for firearms offences, you remain a grave danger to the public.'

Alec Bristow, convicted of conspiracy, was sentenced to 14 years.

Then in 2002 Jones had his conviction quashed by the Court of Appeal when it was found that the trial judge had misdirected the jury over Jones's silence during police questioning. At his retrial at the Old Bailey Jones was reconvicted on all three original charges.

It has been estimated that the cost to the taxpayer of the retrial was £2 million. Ernest Broom, totally innocent in all of this, has received just over £4,000 from the Criminal Injuries

Compensation Authority for the physical and psychological effects of the shooting but he has been forced by mounting debts to sell his Worcester Park home. No longer working, he could not afford to pay his mortgage. What an inadequate response from the authorities for an innocent man shot down by a long-term thug. Peanuts again.

Broom himself has said that he would like to have shown his gratitude to the staff at St Helier Hospital who saved his life. But it was not possible. 'I didn't even have enough money to buy the nurses at the hospital a box of chocolates or a bunch of flowers,' he has said. 'All of those people who worked so hard to save me, all I could say was thank you but it didn't seem enough.'

Addressing Jones at the retrial, Mr Justice Barker commented: 'By some stroke of fate, you got your instructions wrong and Mr Burns was never in your sights. Unfortunately Mr Broom was. It is a miracle that he survived. What you have done, in his words, is to ruin his life.'

'He acted as a good citizen with no thought for himself,' the judge rightly observed. But such an accolade may not be enough to warm Ernest Broom's heart. What on the face of it has elements of farce is in fact a tragedy.

Of Jones and Bristow, the founders of his misfortune, Broom has said with some bitterness: 'They've got free board and lodging. All I was worth was £100 and an old car.'

That must be wrong. And this time it's the authorities paying peanuts.

SWIMMING WITH SHARKS

---❀---

Whitaker Wright swam with sharks in a manner of speaking. But he came to little real harm for he was himself a shark, a larger than life shark, a megalomaniac shark whose end came only when, aging, he could no longer grapple in the deepest waters. Though born in Cheshire, and having spent much of his life in America, he is accounted a Surrey man by virtue of his activities at Witley Park near Guildford and a villainous Surrey shark because of his Stock Exchange finagling. He was so like his near contemporary in Sussex, Horatio Bottomley: able, energetic, ruthless. They both sacrificed others whenever their personal fortunes were threatened. And both men had a desire to put their homes on the map, Bottomley at The Dicker and Whitaker Wright at Witley Park, known in his time, incidentally, as Lea Park.

Wright had made a massive fortune in the United States. He had gone there in 1866, when in his early twenties, as a mining assayer. There is no indication that he had qualified for such work but there can be no doubt that even as a young man he exuded enough confidence to pass as an expert and he had enough intellectual stamina to be able to pick up and assimilate the elements of this complex profession. He was within a short time an ever-present at gold and silver strikes, representing major companies and advising them on the value of new discoveries. And he was in Indian country too in the days when the West was really wild.

Lake Valley in New Mexico was a frontier mining town with all of Hollywood's favourite characters – gamblers, cattle rustlers, dance hall girls, Apache raiders, vigilantes. In 1878 a discovery of rich silver ore, promising 40 ounces to the ton, led to a huge invasion by prospectors. Whitaker Wright and his partner and fellow shark, George Roberts, now promoting stock themselves, sent a colleague, George Daly, to evaluate the deposit. Daly decided that Lake Valley was the ideal site for a stock promotion and bought a huge number of claims. In 1881 Wright went to Lake Valley and with Daly bought even more claims.

But he worked too, his pick in one hand and his gun in the other. 'It was a rough and adventurous life,' we read in Sir Richard Muir's *Memoirs*. 'Once, while prospecting in Idaho, near the Snake River, where the Indians were on the warpath, an Indian and his wife pitched their tents near his hut and he paid them a call. He gave the woman a plug of tobacco, an act which probably saved his life, for shortly afterwards a war party of Indians came to his shanty to kill him, but the squaw who had received the tobacco induced them to leave. They proceeded down the river and massacred three of Whitaker Wright's men.'

It was in the face of such dangers that Whitaker Wright was amassing his first million. Shortly after this event he left for New York and with Roberts established the Sierra Grande Silver Mining Company of Lake Valley. They sent Daly back to Lake Valley where he hired teams of miners to dig shafts. Unfortunately, shortly afterwards, Daly was killed in an ambush by an Apache raiding party.

But this did nothing to deter Wright. On the very day that Daly's body was brought into camp, the first great silver discovery occurred at Lake Valley. Thousands of ounces to the ton, some of the richest ever found, were now being mined. The principal source of this silver was in an underground pocket, 40 feet by 60 feet, known as the Bridal Chamber because of the glistening appearance of its walls by candlelight. They were lined with almost pure silver worth $15,000 and more a ton. The promoters publicised it as the richest silvermine ever discovered, yielding $10 a pound, in an age when the average miner earned $3 a day.

Within a few months over a million dollars in silver was taken out of the Bridal Chamber. Eventually Wright and his partner sold $5 million worth of stock in their Lake Valley mining companies. Roberts' reputation for dishonesty in promoting the stock led to his being forced to sell out his share but at this time no one suspected that Whitaker Wright might not be a man of the utmost probity. He was in fact by now an American citizen, a member of the New York Stock Exchange and chairman of the Philadelphia Mining Executive. But despite all his triumphs as a promoter, by 1889 he had lost much of his fortune – there had been, it seems, 'some trouble with his companies' – and he returned to the United Kingdom, though still retaining an interest in Lake Valley.

What might we have expected a man to do, returning to his homeland after an absence of more than twenty years? Surely it would take him time to find his feet. Surely word was about that here was a man who could make millions but who was not infallible. He could lose money too. It would not be unreasonable to think that investors might just be a touch cautious in their dealings with such a man. Could they, dare they, risk their money with Whitaker Wright? Of course they could. After all, the board of his latest company, London and Globe, included such respectable and reliable figures as Lord Loch, formerly High Commissioner of South Africa, and the Marquess of Dufferin and Ava, the former Governor General of Canada and Viceroy of India. Among other luminaries were Lieutenant General the Honourable S.J. Gough-Calthorpe and Lord Edward Pelham-Clinton. If men such as these trusted Wright, surely he was a man to be relied upon? But perhaps these socially elevated board members had been assured in advance that they would never lose out if things went wrong. And think of the pickings. But what these men with their impressive names and titles seemed to have in common was a complete lack of commercial nous and a willingness to give Wright a totally free hand.

Suffice it to say that within eight years Whitaker Wright was once more a millionaire. Today he would be a multi-millionaire. The Midas touch had not deserted him. By 1897 the *Financial Times* in an article entitled 'Men of Millions' described him as outstanding among international businessmen. And he looked the part, a huge man, with a powerful head, enough to impress those who perhaps wished to be impressed.

It was at this time that Wright acquired from Lord Derby the 9,000 acre Manor of Witley, which extended from Thursley to the Devil's Punchbowl and included Hindhead Common. He pulled down the old manor house and replaced it with the huge Witley Park. Like so many men with a vast fortune and an inflated view of their place in the universal scheme of things, he was in effect building a memorial to himself. We have seen the same kind of vanity in recent times with Nicholas van Hoogstraten's Hamilton Palace at Uckfield in Sussex.

It was, one supposes, a pleasure dome, a building which shouted 'Look at me! Look at my owner!' at all who saw it. For it was magnificent – though not necessarily beautiful – as a building ought to be when it is designed by Lutyens, when it costs £1.85 million and when it takes hundreds of men nearly seven years to build. In addition to its great reception rooms, its 32 bedrooms, its 11 bathrooms – generous provision before the 'en-suite age' – there was a theatre, a conservatory, an observatory with a revolving copper dome. In the huge room he called the Bridal Suite the very dressing table was 32 square feet in size.

Then there were the three artificial lakes, one of them 25 acres in extent, with electric launches as well as rowing and sailing boats. Another was for bathing and the third, the largest, was an ornamental lake with statues, oriental pavilions and fountains, one of which, the dolphin's head fountain, carved from white marble, had been brought from Italy. It was so huge that the railway company refused to transport it from Portsmouth to Haslemere. But men of Whitaker Wright's character are not put off by such inconveniences. He hired a traction engine and a flatbed trailer to bring it to Witley by road. But then they encountered another snag. Arriving at Liphook the contractors found that they could not go under the railway bridge. Again another Whitaker Wright solution. With the permission of the local authority – would anyone dare refuse? – he had the road under the bridge dug out to give enough headroom. Once the dolphin's head was through the road was relaid.

Underneath the largest of the lakes there were grottoes, built of iron and stone, a kind of underwater fairyland. One great chamber of glass, 80 feet in height, was elegantly furnished with a mosaic floor. And just imagine, there was a billiard room down there. One visitor described how 'goldfish come and press their faces against the glass, peering at you with strangely magnified eyes. On summer nights one looks through the green water at the stars and the moon, bright and large, magnified quite ten times by the curved glass and the water.'

Not that this ostentatious extravagance pleased everyone. An article headed 'Despoiling Hindhead Common' in the *Surrey Times* in 1899 reads: 'Many residents of Hindhead are not a little annoyed, and certainly very much grieved, at the poor respect which the new Lord of the Manor is apparently showing for the natural beauty and adornments of Hindhead Common and the Punch Bowl ... Residents have observed the recent visits of gangs of workmen and an "infernal machine" constructed for this special purpose, with trees and bushes lifted bodily from their place with a couple of tons of earth, and carted straight away.' And away the soil was taken to landscape the new Xanadu.

This remarkable enterprise was frequently directed by Whitaker Wright himself, walking his land with a stout oak staff. A lake here, he would order; a mound there; a copse out; another extension. And if the labourers needed to be shown how to work, he'd show them, taking up a pick and shovel himself and going at the task with the fierce energy that he seems to have employed in all his activities.

If some were displeased by the despoiling of the local landscape, however, others in the area were delighted at the arrival of such a vibrant and generous character. He brought work opportunities to many a modest household and money to many a near-empty pocket.

All this time Wright was continuing his vast commercial enterprises on the London Stock Exchange, promoting mining ventures throughout the world. During these years, rich gold discoveries were being made, particularly in Australia, and Wright, knowledgeable, astute and undeniably ruthless, made immense profits.

But then his companies began to falter yet again. Lake Valley, that goldmine of a silvermine, could no longer sustain its initial output and Wright held back his on-the-spot manager's reports lest there should be a panic and consequent falls in share prices. But it was not only from America that troubled notes came. The Boer War had a significant effect upon the finance and commodity markets and again mining ventures were imperilled. By 1899, Whitaker Wright's various interests were in serious trouble.

And the other sharks swam around, waiting their turn. Just as Wright during his great years had done when he had spotted some vulnerable but weakening rival. Wright's plans to invest in the building of the projected Bakerloo railway line were abandoned.

By December 1900 he was denounced at the London and Globe AGM for misusing invested funds. He was to become a pariah when it was found that he had divested himself of the majority of his shares and invested his profits in significant property holdings in the London area. An official enquiry revealed that the deficiency in his companies totalled about £7.5 million. Those whose investments had failed now demanded that he be prosecuted. But Wright fought on, continued putting on a brave front, defying his critics, but one by one his companies collapsed. In 1902, after hiding in the ice-house at Witley Park for a week, he fled to the United States under an assumed name. But a warrant awaited his arrival.

Some months later Wright was extradited from America and returned to Britain to face trial in 1904 for fraud. The case revealed a trail of deceit, misinformation, fraudulent accounting, all within the framework of company promotions, and a series of gigantic operations on the Stock Exchange.

The charges might be summarised as knowingly making false statements with the intention of defrauding shareholders and creditors. It was a highly complex case and for ten days the jury struggled to understand the machinations of the Stock Exchange, the workings of high powered companies and in particular the sharp practice of Whitaker Wright. The court heard of a whole complex range of borrowings, lendings, purchases and sales. Often the text used had been completely baffling but there was no doubt that to the very end Wright had given shareholders and directors false information about the state of the company, telling them that the London and Globe balance sheet was excellent, exaggerating its assets and their value.

And how Wright wriggled, alleging under cross-examination that the alterations in the 1900 balance sheet must have been done by the accountants. And what an almost impenetrable balance sheet it was, with money in the Globe account passing through several of Wright's other companies before ending up at its final resting place. At that time, so he said, he was fully occupied with other major matters and gave no personal attention to the balance sheet.

At the end of the ten-day trial, held not in a Criminal Court but in the Civil Law Courts in the Strand, Mr Justice Bigham, was to congratulate the jury on having reached the final stage of a

Whitaker Wright (centre) in court.

wearisome case. Even he, an experienced commercial judge, wryly admitted that he had found it highly intricate.

After being sentenced to seven years' imprisonment and before being taken off to prison, Wright went down to the private room that he had occupied throughout the trial – for arrangements in the Civil Court were different from those in other courts – to discuss matters with counsel and friends. He had the air of a man still confident and full of fight, speaking with assurance about the probability of the reduction of his sentence and even of the possibility of a retrial.

But Whitaker Wright had a taste for the dramatic. The *Surrey Advertiser* describes the last act of his drama. After a visit to the lavatory, Wright returned to the consultation room. 'He asked for a cigar, and one was given him from his own case. A match was struck, and he was about to light the cigar, when he commenced to breathe heavily and sank into a chair. A doctor was sent for but a short examination convinced him that death was imminent. Within a quarter of an hour of his being taken ill, he ceased to breathe.'

He had, while in the lavatory, taken a cyanide capsule. That he intended suicide if he were found guilty cannot be doubted. A loaded revolver, fully cocked, was found in the hip pocket of his trousers.

After Wright's death the Witley Park property was broken up and Hindhead Common and the Devil's Punchbowl bought for the National Trust. Witley Park remains but Wright's house burnt down in 1952.

Appropriately enough, it seems, another shark, the American subway magnate, Charles Tyson Yerkes, who himself had been gaoled for fraud, and who described his business methods simply as 'buy up old junk, fix it up a little and load it upon other fellows,' took over the Bakerloo railway project.

Fraudster or not, let it be remembered that not everyone in Surrey disapproved of Whitaker Wright. Indeed, he was loved in the Witley area and there was a great outpouring of grief when the news of his death reached the district. Many locals attended his funeral, arguing that he had brought them work, that he was a generous benefactor. The *Morning Post* attested to this: 'The village of Witley, where the kindness and generosity of the dead man are held in high appreciation, closed its shutters out of respect and sympathy. Villagers, who came from far and near, carried in their hands bunches of violets from the neighbouring lanes and copses ... these simple blossoms were laid reverently on the mound which marks the earthly resting place.' At least, local people said, he had never robbed them. But then, they had no money to lose.

BIBLIOGRAPHY

———————— ✿ ————————

Bebbington, W. *Rogues Go Racing* Good and Betts (undated)
Darbyshire, Neil and Hilliard, Brian *The Flying Squad* Headline (1993)
Greeno, Edward *War on the Underworld* John Long (1960)
Hart, Edward T. *Britain's Godfather* True Crime Library (1993)
Jennings, Andrew, Lashmar, Paul and Simson, Vyv *Scotland Yard's Cocaine Connection* Arrow Books (1991)
Morton, James *Gangland 1* Little, Brown (1992)
Morton, James *Gangland 2* Little, Brown (1994)
Morton, James *Supergrasses and Informers* Little, Brown (1995)
Muir, Richard *Memoirs* John Lane (1926)
Roberts, Tom *Friends and Villains* Hodder and Stoughton (1987)
Slipper, Jack *Slipper of the Yard* Sidgwick and Jackson (1981)

The author has also consulted many national and local newspapers as well as crime magazines.